For Stan,

my best friend, lover, and outdoor companion

for a quarter century.

. . . .

© 1997 Christine L. Thomas
Illustrations © Paige Moriarty
Published by Falcon Press® Publishing Co., Inc.
Helena and Billings, Montana

First Edition

Design, typesetting, and other prepress work
by Falcon Press, Helena, Montana.
Dust jacket art and all inside illustrations by Paige Moriarty.
Printed in the United States of America.

Library of Congress Cataloging-in-Publication Data

Thomas, Christine, 1951-
     Becoming an outdoors woman : my outdoor adventure / Christine
Thomas. — 1st ed.
         p.   cm.
     ISBN 1-56044-526-2
     1. Hunting—Anecdotes. 2. Fishing—Anecdotes. 3. Thomas,
Christine. 1951-   . I. Title.
SK33.T45   1997
796.5'092—dc21
     [B]   96-47789
                                                                CIP

Contents

. . . .

Preface

. . . .

Professionally, I am a professor in the College of Natural Resources of the University of Wisconsin-Stevens Point. In my professor life, I have four jobs to do. I arm graduate and undergraduate students with the skills to be responsible stewards of our natural resources. I do my part to maintain the university by serving in various faculty governance roles. I conduct research. I extend the knowledge of the university to the community through outreach programming and participation in policy making.

In 1990, as a relatively new professor, I was still searching for my niche in the outreach area. That year, Dr. Raymond Anderson, professor of wildlife at Stevens Point, and Dr. Robert Jackson, professor of psychology at the University of Wisconsin-LaCrosse, invited me to participate in an outreach project that would change the course of my life. That project was a workshop called "Breaking Down Barriers to Participation of Women in Angling and Hunting." The audience for the workshop was state agency personnel and conservation club leaders.

The group generated a list of twenty-one barriers to participation. Most of the barriers related to not having had the chance in childhood to learn outdoor skills. I thought we could break down that barrier.

As a result, we developed a three-day workshop to teach women skills needed for hunting, fishing, camping, and other outdoor pursuits. That workshop, "Becoming an Outdoors-Woman (BOW)," was held for the first time in Wisconsin in 1991. Today, the concept has proven so popular that forty states and four Canadian provinces will offer the workshop to an estimated six thousand women.

I am often asked if I started the workshop as a result of a burning passion to help women move outdoors. That was not the case. While I had been actively involved in women's issues in resource management professions, and while I was actively involved in the outdoors, I did not see the "Becoming an Outdoors-Woman" program as a mission. It began as an interesting project that I could use to fulfill the outreach component of my work. It grew into a mission.

Along the way, the idea of this book began to take shape. I have a friend who helped with a number of workshops in the early years of this project. Tammy Peterson, who worked for the Wisconsin Department of Natural Resources and later the Fish and Wildlife Service, was one of the co-authors of the planning guide that state agencies use to plan workshops. In the spring of 1993, we spoke at the Western Bowhunting Conference in Bozeman, Montana. Instead of staying at the conference site, we rented a cabin out in the mountains (Tammy's idea). Every night when the conference ended, we drove to Yellowstone to enjoy the spring wildlife until dark. We would stay up talking half the night. We talked about the idea of writing books about our outdoor adventures. One of the ideas we came up with was an evening program on how to tell outdoor stories. We piloted the idea at the Wisconsin BOW that year. I told "The Aqua Velva Man." The audience just roared. Some of the women laughed till the tears fell. I became hooked on the audience reaction. I knew that they understood the emotions and the humor in the story. That is when I knew I would actually write this book.

While working on the BOW program across the country, I have developed many friendships. Two of those friends, Gloria Erickson and Charmaine Adolph Wargolet, were the first two women I called when I returned from the Idaho elk hunt. They were the first two with whom I shared "The Cycle of the Hunt." They listened and understood as I told the story, blubbering away on the phone. Many women don't have close female friends to share their outdoor adventures with. I am blessed to have those two. I have enjoyed sharing their adventures as well.

I love to tell stories. Stan, my husband, has sure had to listen to his share of them. While writing this book, I needed to share the chapters for confirmation that I was on the right track. Stan and my friend Diane Lueck were the sounding boards. Stan listened politely and Diane was the steadfast encourager. At each juncture where I might quit, she came up with just the right words to keep me going. When I got "stuck" in some quagmire, she came up with just the right advice to pry me loose. I appreciate all this very much.

Of course I appreciate all the friends who populate the stories, my partners in my quest to become an outdoorswoman.

When I started the BOW program, I did not even recognize that I had also faced barriers in getting involved in outdoor activities. I had been introduced to the outdoors by the two most important men in my life, my father and husband. I had been encouraged by other important men: Uncle Harry, the consummate outdoorsman; Dan Trainer, the second dad; colleagues with whom I have worked through the years. I have had excellent female outdoor companions: Elaine Kalmbacher, Pat Empson, Shannon Thomas. I ignored the barriers, at least on the face of things.

But, the barriers were there too. The ill fitting clothing. The guide who thought you shouldn't be there. The press of professional, personal, and financial responsibilities. The biggest barriers, however, have been the ones that I created in my own head. I bet that is true for most people.

My hope for this book is that you will read it and see yourselves, both men and women. I hope you will catch a line or an image and that there will be a connection between us, if only for these few chapters. I hope that those who are trying to become outdoorswomen and outdoorsmen will be encouraged to continue. I hope that I will make you laugh and that the shared experience of the laughter will strengthen our bond in the outdoor community.

Rite of Passage

. . . .

I sat quietly on the rickety wooden dock in front of the house in the after-midnight darkness. The light from my folks' cigarettes glowed from inside the screened-in front porch. The mosquitoes buzzed incessantly, drowned out periodically by the late summer hum of cicadas. The odor of mosquito repellent hung around me like a shroud.

When the fish hit this ten-year-old's line, she thought she was being pulled in the water. As fast as it hit, the fish leaped into the air directly in front of me. When it surfaced, its head was actually above mine, its tail still submerged. The mammoth animal disappeared below the surface and ran.

"Daddy, Daddy, help!" I yelled frantically, as the water from the murky canal ran off me, down the dock, and back to its source.

My dad came running out the front door and down the steps. Meanwhile, that fish was stripping line off my reel like there was no drag whatsoever. My dad covered the few steps to the waterfront just in time to see the end of my line reflected in the moonlight as it went under the wooden walking bridge 100 yards up the canal. When the line came to the knot on the reel, the line snapped off and the monster was gone.

"Must have been one of those big old German browns," my dad opined.

I fished, therefore I was. In fact, I don't remember when I was not. I suppose it was natural, given my early days growing up in a tiny house situated on a canal that flowed into Cass Lake in southeastern Michigan. I began by fishing from the dock. My sister, Debra, and I both had old casting rods with black string tied to the ends. We used everything imaginable for bait: crawlers, minnows, bacon, bread, hot dogs, even cheese. We caught gills, bullheads, perch, and once even a walleye (which was a major neighborhood event).

Debra and I were two of the early tournament anglers. We always had a summer-long fishing contest with Lou Ashbeck, our next-door neighbor. It was a mission every summer. That is probably one reason I was still out fishing after midnight. We never lost. Lou went down to defeat by at least a thousand fish each year. Of course, he rarely put a line in the water. We fished continuously, never certain we would win until the summer ended with the start of school.

Debra never really did that much fishing, because she did not like to bait the hook or take off the fish. I would have done it for her, and probably did, but I am sure that our father, Ken Zube, would not. So, first born that I was and willing to do the dirty work, I became the only son. The fishing companion. The rabid Detroit Tiger fan. Fishing in the morning and evening, baseball in the afternoon. Bass and batting averages.

It is a funny thing, actually, that interests that were initially sparked as a way of relating to my father ended up to be greater passions for me than for him.

Take baseball, for instance. At age six I was often asked to umpire baseball games at recess. The reason? I knew the rules better than anyone else. Eventually I knew the rules better than my dad. There were many things like that. We would argue.

"That kid would rather be right than president," my dad would say of me when I insisted on the facts I had tried so hard to learn because he was interested in the subject.

He was right about me. It is sad actually. When the student outdistanced the professor, distance came into the relationship. I never did learn to keep my mouth shut and just let him be right. What real difference could it have made in the end?

By high school I was listening to every game on the radio that was not televised. I was in love with Denny McLain. I dreamed of being a baseball announcer, thinking foolishly that it was just slightly more plausible than actually being a professional player or owning a professional team.

It seems strange to me that my dad never took me to a game. When I was thirteen years old, Walter Poe, the eighth-grade history teacher, offered to take the top student from each class to a Detroit Tiger game. I set out to win. The last week of the contest found Jack Short and me tied for first place. Poe posed a tie-breaking trivia question. We hit the library with a vengeance. Whoever delivered the answer first, after the last bell of the day, was the winner.

We both had the correct answer. We both had the same last class. The running distance was equal, but short, pudgy Christine could never outrun short, skinny Jack. She would have to outsmart him.

The bell rang. Jack ran up the sidewalk and down the hall. I cut across the courtyard and yelled the answer in the open window. I won. Jack punched me in the arm, leaving a nasty bruise. Mr. Poe took both of us to the game.

What I remember most about the game was the vivid green color of the field, the bright uniforms, the smell of hot dogs and popcorn, and the sound of the vendors. It is only recently that I figured out why the game looked so vivid. It was because we had a black-and-white television. It was the first game that I ever saw in color.

Somewhere along the line, Dad bought me my first spinning rod and reel. The reel was a handsome metallic green. It said, "Mark something or other" on it. I remember him showing me how to hold the rod with the stem of the reel between my middle fingers. "That way it won't get away from you," he counseled. I still hold my fishing rod that way today, whether trolling, casting, or still-fishing. I always think of him when I assume that grip.

Our Saturday and Sunday routine of strikes on and off the diamond worked well enough when I was smaller. But little girls become bigger girls, and bigger girls get bigger ideas. I decided I would like to fish on weekdays as well. This would require boat privileges. We had a small Starcraft aluminum boat with a $3^1/2$-horsepower Johnson Seahorse motor. Why do I remember those details? Some years later I bought a boat and motor for my husband, Stan, and cannot remember the make of either component.

But in Ken Zube's eyes boat privileges were a rite of passage and therefore required a test. The test was swimming halfway across the lake at its widest point. I can't tell you the distance, but it was WIDE.

I practiced all the first part of that summer. I was probably about eleven years old, because I remember achieving the level of Yellow Cap in swimming at Camp Sherwood Girl Scout Camp in Lapeer. Surely *that* level of expertise would equip me with the strength to make the swim. When I arrived home from camp, I announced my intention to "take the test."

The following Saturday morning, early, before water skiers and wind, we headed out onto the lake. My dad ran the boat and I shivered nervously in my bathing suit. The water was steel gray, a reflection of the overcast sky. The atmosphere was heavy and smelled of outboard fuel mixed faintly with dead fish. When we reached the mid-point in the widest part of the lake, I plunged over the gunwale and began swimming. He rowed alongside.

It seemed to me that the water was a great deal colder out there in the middle. Surely the imagined snapping turtles beneath me must be the size of hula hoops. At least that was what Lou Ashbeck (the fishing tournament loser) used to say. He used to tell stories about a water skier who went down on the lake and was eaten by giant turtles. I don't know how many martinis it took to fuel that story, but it didn't take any to believe it.

I flunked the test. Somewhere past the mid-point, the cold, exhaustion, and fear got hold of me and my dad had to haul me in. Disappointment does not begin to describe how I felt as I sat in the bow and cried as we motored toward home.

Some tears may fall along the outdoor trail, as they may fall along any path where striving is required. I recently saw a woman quoted as being contemptuous of women who cry. Of course almost everyone in our society is contemptuous of men who cry, as though experiencing the range of your feelings as a living, breathing person is inherently bad. We have moved our physical and psychological selves indoors to a more comfortable climate and along the way have lost important elements of who we are. There is no sin in feeling or expressing disappointment. The sin is in wallowing in it.

So the practicing continued. I went to the beach daily. I swam out to the diving raft and back, over and over. I finally passed the test. Why don't I remember that day?

What I do remember is taking the boat out by myself that first time. It was early on a weekday morning. My dad went to work. I headed out on the lake. It was like glass. I put a silver-and-black Rapala, a lure about three inches long that looks like a minnow, on my line and trolled the edge of a weed bed that I had often admired but that we had rarely fished. I hadn't made one pass and I had a strike. It felt like a whale. It dragged out line. I horsed it back. It came leaping out of the water. I am sure I whooped and hollered (most of my fishing companions do not like this characteristic). Miraculously, everything held together. I landed about a sixteen-inch smallmouth. What a trophy! In those days, we did catch-and-release, but there was nothing altruistic in the gesture. I think my dad did not want to bother with cleaning the fish. We did have a stringer in the tackle box, however. I could not release this one until my dad got home. That poor fish must have spent a very long day. He did swim away after he was shown off in the late afternoon.

Hoppe's NO. 9
· ·

I never had a chance to hunt as a child, but hunting was certainly part of my early remembrances. What parents do shapes future adults, even though some years may pass before the early planted seeds bear fruit.

My dad hunted. I would not call him a hunter—that is, someone for whom hunting is a defining life activity. Rather, he hunted recreationally, on occasion, the way some people play miniature golf. Nevertheless, he owned a shotgun, a rifle, and an assortment of handguns.

As a very small child, I would accompany my dad and mother to shoot trap. We didn't go to a range. In those days, Detroit had not yet moved as far as West Bloomfield. Urban sprawl had not desecrated every last inch of open landscape. There were still many undeveloped farm fields. We took a hand thrower and went to one of those fields to shoot. My parents would take turns throwing for each other.

I do not think of my mother as an outdoorswoman. Oh, she did take her turn as a Girl Scout leader the year Debra's troop needed one. She went to camp, even winter camp. That was being a good mother, not an outdoorswoman. Still, she had her own shotgun, a .410.

"Darlene is a really good shot," I remember my dad saying.

I know that those words spoken admiringly of my mother made me want to be a good shot as well.

There is often a special relationship between dads and oldest daughters. Dad is the first man you ever love. That is not to say that you always get along. Maybe you never get along. Still, what he is and what he does has a huge influence on what you define as "maleness" for the rest of your life.

In our situation, there were no sons. In addition to being the oldest daughter, I was also the only son. If a "dad activity" was underway, I wanted to be in on it. When he and my mother shot trap, I collected the missed clay targets so they could pitch them again.

We had a black-and-white springer spaniel, AKC Kit of Cass Lake. Kit was a pheasant dog deluxe according to my dad, and a garbage hound, beggar, and neighborhood menace according to my mother. I never got to go hunting with them, but they generally came back with birds, if that says anything for the dog.

It was with Kit that I forged my first real relationship with a dog. When Kit was a puppy, she ventured out on the spring ice on the canal in front of our house. The ice gave way and she fell through. By some miracle, my mother happened to see her, crawled out on the cracking ice, and, using an oar, lifted the pup to safety. Kit never forgot the terror of that situation. If I fished from shore, she would lie between me

and the water. If I went to the beach to swim, Kit had to be confined to the house. Whenever she escaped, she would track me to the beach, splash out into the water, grab my arm firmly in her mouth, and drag me onto the shore. That resulted in me sputtering, scolding, and crying as I dragged her back to the house.

Besides pheasant hunting, the only other hunting I remember my dad doing was a mule deer and antelope hunt in Wyoming. He went with friends from work. That was the only time he ever took a vacation without my mother. I thought that trip was a really big deal. He took slides of the trip. Those were the first slides I ever saw, and I devoured every scene and hung on every description. A few years later, when we started doing reports on states in school, I did mine on Wyoming. Many years later my husband and I took our first out-of-state vacation to Wyoming. Forty years later I can still tell you that the outfitter my dad hunted with was named L. D. Fromme. I was the only one in the family who liked the venison. I still love it.

As Kit aged, my dad used that as an excuse to quit hunting. She still wanted to go. The opening day of pheasant season, each October, she would whine by the back door all day.

Even though Dad lost interest in hunting, he remained interested in guns. In my teenage years, he would take me to the shooting range to shoot handguns. After shooting, we would get out the Hoppe's NO. 9 to clean them. Anyone who has ever spent much time around guns knows the oily feel and the strong, pungent, petroleum-based odor. I know it can't be good for you, but I love the smell. It conjures up springer spaniels, pheasant feathers, and an ornery old pipefitter who introduced his daughter to guns, gun dogs, and hunting, even though she never went on the hunt. I always thought Hoppe's would make "killer" aftershave. I couldn't imagine being seriously interested in a man who didn't smell like Hoppe's once in a while.

Becoming a
Farm Woman

. . . .

I met Stan during my sophomore year at Central Michigan University. We were both biology majors. That was probably the only thing we had in common. While I was certainly an angler, no amount of imagination could be summoned up that would envision me as an outdoorswoman. Stan, on the other hand, wasn't much of a fisherman, but his experiences as a farmer, hunter, and Green Beret put him so far into the outdoorsman category as to be somewhat intimidating.

A few months after we began dating, we took a drive up to his Uncle Harry's cabin on Devils' Bend Creek, near Grayling. I don't know why we went there, since we did not have a key to the place. I guess it must have just been a Sunday drive. The snow was very deep, so we had to walk to the cabin. I did not own a pair of boots of any kind. I wore a pair of jeans, with nylons for socks, and a pair of flimsy sneakers. With each step I sunk into the crusted snow. The snow soaked my sneakers and the ice cut my ankles. I had neither gloves nor hat. It was our first north woods experience together. I remember it as an ordeal, because I wasn't prepared with the proper clothing.

Late that summer, I went to Lawrence to stay with Stan's family. I had had very little farm experience. What little I had was not positive. All I knew of farm life was that my dairy farmer aunt and uncle had taken me under their wings while my mother was hospitalized during the birth of my sister. I had been homesick, so they had taken this not-quite-three-year-old out to the barn to see the new calves. I had become so enthralled with the furry beasts that in my zeal to get closer I fell into the manure gutter. My aunt hosed me down thoroughly with the cold water normally reserved for the garden before scrubbing me from stem to stern in the tub. It was all I could think about on the eve of my trip to the Thomas farm. The thought conjured up the pungent smell of silage and the earthy smell of cow manure. To say I was not a farm girl was a gross understatement.

The Thomases were horse people. They owned a number of saddle and draft horses. When I first arrived, Stan took me to a western store to outfit me for my first horseback riding experience. He bought me a pair of western boots and a pair of leather gloves. Both were very well made, and the price of them was more money than I made in a week at my summer job. I protested such an expensive gift. Besides, I had only seen such boots on the likes of Porter Wagoner as he crooned country music on television. I was a sixties girl and would not want to be caught dead in anything Porter Wagoner might wear.

"If you are going to be involved in activities, you need to have the proper equipment. Cheap junk and equipment that does not fit is dangerous and interferes with the activity," Stan lectured.

It was good advice. Through the years, any piece of outdoor equipment that Stan has given to me has been the best or better than he could afford. I still have almost all of it.

So I took the generous gift and thoroughly enjoyed my first horseback riding experience. Actually, I was very nervous sitting there on top of that horse. It was so big compared to me. They do tend to have minds of their own. It was a mixture of excitement and apprehension that I felt.

I thoroughly enjoyed the whole visit. The farm was a new and engaging place. August is the height of the garden season. The minutes-old sweet corn, tomatoes, and other goodies, along with farm-raised beef, were treats that I had never experienced. The hospitality and warmth of the family were wonderful.

Some months later, when Stan and I announced our intention to get married, I am sure that everyone wondered if I would make it on the farm. However, they liked me and they are good people, so they did all they could to help me. For my part, I am no quitter, so I did the best I could to fit in.

You may be wondering what becoming a farm woman has to do with becoming an outdoorswoman. I maintain that those women who were raised on farms probably have a leg up on the rest of us in the outdoorswoman department. If you are farming and are involved in the day-to-day work of the farm, you learn many things that you might not learn in suburbia. You certainly learn a broader range of skills. You learn early on how to dress for the elements. You learn how to fix things. You learn how to operate power equipment, how to pull trailers and wagons, and how to be more self-reliant. The rhythms of farm life tie you more closely to the natural cycles of life and death. You see more wildlife and consequently learn more about it.

I like to think I became a farm woman. My mother-in-law taught me how to garden, an activity that I did with a vengeance. One year, for instance, I had three hundred tomato plants and a fifty-foot (yes, that is 50) row of zucchini. Just imagine that! What on earth would you do with a fifty-foot row of zucchini? When Stan was just about to divorce me over one more serving of zucchini (it would have been grounds, I would agree), I decided to load up the pickup and take them to the neighbor's hogs. I did that day after day, until finally the neighbor asked me to stop bringing them, because the hogs were refusing to eat any more.

I tried everything I could that I thought was farm woman-like. I canned, quilted, baked, cooked for large family gatherings, rode and raised horses, even took up listening to country music (might as well have the music to go with the boots). I disced and plowed and hauled manure. I hauled supper to the field and baled hay. I loved listening to the family and neighborhood stories. I hope that I became a farm woman in my attitude toward others as well as in my activities.

Skipper
. . . .

If you are really lucky, somewhere along the outdoor trail you will experience one of the most satisfying relationships you will ever have in your life. That relationship will be with an individual who worships the ground you walk on, who loves you even when you are mean and ugly, who will try to please you no matter how much effort that takes, and who lives to share your outdoor adventures. I had one of those relationships. It lasted eleven beautiful years. My partner in that relationship was a scruffy-looking Airedale terrier named Skipper—Bear-Dale Skipper, according to his AKC registration.

Just a few short weeks after Stan and I were married, we took part of our wedding-present money and drove to Grand Rapids, Michigan, and bought that black-and-tan bundle of energy for one hundred dollars. It may be the best one hundred dollars that we ever spent.

Skipper was our only child for ten years. He went nearly everywhere we did. He understood everything we said. He had all the stereotypical Airedale terrier personality characteristics, both good and bad. He had incredible energy and stamina, keen intelligence, unfailing loyalty, and tremendous courage. His varmint-dog instincts also drove him to fight with any nonhuman animal no matter what its size, defenses, or disposition.

My first outdoor experience with Skipper was a hike. It came during one of those characteristic southwestern Michigan February thaws. One boring afternoon, this still-unemployed recent college graduate newlywed decided to take the dog for a walk over to where Stan worked. If we didn't make the three- or four-mile hike before Stan left work, I figured he would pick us up on his way home. We headed out in the sunny, mid to late afternoon. Skipper bounced along beside me on his new leash. The snow was melting and the roadside was wet with meltwaters of the mini-glaciers that had been formed by the winter's snowplow deposits.

The walk was longer than I had judged. Before we were halfway to our destination, the sun was slipping low on the horizon and the temperature was dropping rapidly. Little Skipper, only a three-month-old pup, was beginning to tire. His feet were wet and he was getting cold. I had not considered the capabilities of my outdoor companion when I set out on the adventure. I took off my coat and removed a sweatshirt that I was wearing. After replacing my coat, I lifted my shivering charge (who, while not yet half-grown, still weighed nearly twenty pounds), wrapped him in the sweatshirt, and carried him the rest of the way.

If you look through our photo album for the first ten years' worth of pictures, Skipper is there in nearly all our adventures. He loved to fish, for instance. He was a better companion for some types of fishing than for others. Stream fishing was not good. You couldn't keep him out of the stream, so whoever he accompanied did not have a chance of catching anything.

He was a pro at fishing from a boat. I loved to take him along. He'd jump into the boat as soon as you started loading up the fishing tackle. He would take his place in the bottom of the boat and sit fairly quietly until you got a strike. Then he would jump up, front paws on the gunwale, dark eyes focused keenly at the water surface, intent as a German shorthair pointer on a bird, body fairly vibrating with anticipation. As soon as the fish was in the boat, the tension broke and Skipper would come over to investigate, tail wagging and nose twitching.

He wasn't a half-bad bird dog either. Those early days in the 1970s were wonderful pheasant years in southwestern Michigan. My in-laws, Lee and Anita Thomas, have a beautiful farm there. Skipper and I had the run of the place.

He didn't have a nose, really, but he made up for that with his keen eyesight and his desire to please. I am convinced that he saw the birds before he smelled them. He would range out in front of you, back and forth across the field with his head up, looking all the while. When he spotted a bird, his whole body would go instantly tense, tail erect, and every muscle quivering. He was a flusher, not a pointer, so you had to be ready all the time.

He loved to road hunt too. This is not as bad as it sounds, because we never actually shot at anything. Skipper was always with us in the truck. Stan drove with Skipper sitting on the right and me in the middle. All you had to say was, "Pheasant!" When Skip would spot the bird walking along the road, he would come unglued.

One day I had him "up on the muck," a forty-acre piece of my in-laws' farm that was adjacent to Uncle Rog's and Aunt Marie's place. It was a good place to look for birds because the low ground around a pond on the piece was in permanent cover. We tripped a rooster loose out of that cover and the bird sailed across the fence line onto Rog's side. Skipper scooted under the barbed wire after the cackling bird, only to find himself the center of attention of the dozen or so mare ponies and foals that Rog had. Skipper was surrounded. Those mares formed a circle around him and they were closing in. He looked at those mares, then he looked at me. "Get the heck out of there," I yelled.

He turned tail and streaked between two oncoming mares, under the fence, and over to my side.

I can't begin to say how many skunks he tangled with over the years. It didn't matter how badly he was sprayed, he attacked the next skunk with equal vigor. What a mess! The first time this happened, we were collecting maple sap on Stan's grandparents', Earl and Ethyl Thomas, farm. Skipper enjoyed those outings a great deal. As we followed the horse-drawn sap tank down through the woods, we smelled that familiar odor and saw Skipper rolling on the ground, pawing his face. We never did see the skunk. Stan mentioned that he had heard that tomato juice worked to get rid of the smell, so Aunt Marie gave us a case of home-canned juice. Skipper looked pretty pathetic sitting there in the bathtub, tomato juice slathered all over, with chunks of celery sticking to his hair. The tomato juice helped, but for months after, whenever his coat became damp, you would have a chance to remember the skunk.

We took him nearly everywhere with us. On one trip to Wyoming, we sneaked him into a motel at night. He was well behaved and almost never barked, so this wasn't a problem until we woke in the morning. The maids had set up a table outside our door and were folding linens. We were on the second floor, so the window was not an option. What to do about getting the dog outside? Stan solved the problem by emptying out a duffel and zipping the dog inside. It was one of those square olive-drab army duffels that parachutes come packed in. It had two handles on

the top. I can still see Stan walking past those maids, carrying the duffel by the handles, with the dog's feet kicking at the sides of the canvas.

Skipper loved going to the Upper Peninsula to our cabin. The yard was full of red squirrels, which he enjoyed chasing. One day, when Skip was about nine years old, he went streaking across the yard after one of the nimble little critters. Suddenly Skip just fell over on his side. I became hysterical and yelled for help. "He passed out. He passed out," I cried.

My sister, a nurse, and her husband, Dave, a paramedic, came running with their medical bags. They thought I was yelling about Stan. After a few minutes the dog got up but was very weak. Three veterinarians, an EKG, and a chest x-ray later, we determined that Skipper had damaged the valves in his heart, probably in a serious illness he had had as a pup. Sometimes he would run faster than his weakened heart could pump blood. Then he would just fall over. We were able to regulate the difficulty somewhat with medication, but he deteriorated steadily after the cabin incident.

One hot July day, we came home to find him lying on a rug in the garage, too weak to get up. I tried to feed and water him by hand, to no avail. Our vet was out of town and we probably would not have wanted to subject our pet to the ride to Stevens Point anyway. We both knew what had to be done. Stan carried Skipper out behind the barn. I was too much of a coward to go along. While I stood in the driveway crying, the shot rang out. I cried aloud in anguish. Stan buried our friend beneath an oak near the barn.

Besides being a loyal friend, Skipper was a wonderful outdoor companion. He gave me the courage to go places and do things that I might have feared doing alone. We made wonderful memories together and he is still missed over a decade later.

The Open-Air Camp

. . . .

The first fall after we were married, Uncle Rog and Stan's dad went deer hunting in the Upper Peninsula of Michigan. Stan wanted to go, but I pitched a fit about taking separate vacations. I feel bad about that now, because I wish he had gone with them so that he would have that positive interaction in his storehouse of memories. On the other hand, because I felt guilty about his not having had the opportunity to go, I engineered a deer hunting excursion for the two of us the next year. That trip ignited what has turned out to be a lifelong passion.

Stan's family hunted for decades in what used to be known as the Ford River State Forest, not far from the town of Ralph. That tiny Upper Peninsula community had a store, last known as Palluconi's General Store; a tavern, still known as the Hunter's Bar; a Post Office; and a tiny little church. The economy of Ralph was based on pulp cutting, mining, hunting, and snowmobiling. During the deer season an entrepreneurial local would set up a card table on Ralph's four corners and sell Upper Peninsula delicacies known as pasties. These were basically beef (or perhaps venison) pot pies with assorted fall vegetables. One pastie would stick with you for at least two days.

George Brown, the owner of a sport shop in Stan's home town (both George and the shop were long dead before I arrived in Lawrence), is reputed to have been the first of the local deer hunters to venture to Ralph. Over the years, more and more men (and a few wives) from the community ventured to the area. Whenever talk of deer hunting came up, the talk was about Ralph and the stories that were generated over the years. I don't know why, but I love to hear these stories, many of them about people I never knew. I was pretty well pumped up with the stories long before we headed north for my first deer hunt.

We planned to **camp** in the back of the truck, a Chevy 4x4 that we used for our farming activities. We purchased a cap that was well finished inside for the back of the truck. We put curtains on the windows, built a bunk in the back, bought Eddie Bauer goose down sleeping bags that zipped together (hey, we had been married less than two years), and began to assemble the necessary gear.

Earlier in the year, Stan gave me my first rifle. It was an old Marlin lever-action in .35 Remington caliber. Dick Kroeg, the local barber, had a shooting range on his place, and we went over there to sight in my gift. That was the first rifle shooting I ever had the opportunity to do. I loved that gun. I am a person who becomes really attached to the equipment I use. I always think that what I have is the best. It is difficult to talk me into changing once I become attached. Stan gave me a nifty braided leather sling to put on the gun. The next year, I bought all the necessary gun refinishing products and reblued the metal parts and refinished the wood. After that, I thought it was the most beautiful firearm in the world.

Michigan's deer season is always the same, November 15 through the end of the month. We decided to head north for the Thanksgiving week, so we would only need to take one week off from work. The preparations began weeks in advance. Our dining room became a repository for all the many items that would be needed and many items that would not be needed.

When the appointed day of departure arrived, the entire cargo area was loaded to the roof. In addition, Stan had built a plywood box that looked much like a coffin. That was tied to the top of the cap. It is where we stored the paraphernalia that you always hope you don't need: tire chains, jack, etc. We loaded Skipper in the truck and headed north.

I love to go "up north." I loved it in Michigan and I still love it in Wisconsin. As the farms melt away and the forest becomes the predominant landscape, I begin to feel excitement and exhilaration. There seem to be more possibilities and more variety of wildlife to be enjoyed.

One of the possibilities when you head north in Michigan is the Mackinac Bridge. I crossed it as a child the year it opened. On this trip it was dark when we approached the bridge, so it was lit in all its night-time glory. I am always excited to see the bridge. Somehow I feel some ownership in it. I will admit to being somewhat of a chicken when it comes to high places, so I find myself leaning involuntarily toward the center of the vehicle when we drive across.

The plan was to stay in Escanaba overnight and head to the woods in the morning. We arrived in Escanaba late and found a motel on the outskirts of town. I moved our bags into the room and Stan took Skipper for a run before bed. There was a vacant field adjacent to the motel that looked like a likely spot. Skipper took off full speed across the field but didn't go twenty-five yards before he fell to the ground, kicking his feet in the air and biting at his legs. Stan ran over to see what the problem might be, only to find that Skipper had run headlong into the worst stand of burdock that you can imagine. He was completely covered from head to toe by the round, sticker-like seeds. The more he thrashed, the worse things became. Airedales have bushy beards and eyebrows. The beard was completely matted and his eyes were stuck shut. Stan had to carry him out of the field and into the motel room. We put him in the bathtub, where we could contain the mess. I sacrificed my comb and brush and we went to work on him. Hours and many wastebaskets full of burrs later, we went to bed. It felt like the picky little burr stickers were poking into my body everywhere. My hands were raw and red from the ordeal. Skipper seemed unaffected by the whole thing. So much for one last romantic night in town.

Did I mention that we were planning to **camp**? The last camping that I had done had been as a girl scout. In our troop, winter camping meant going to Camp Sherwood and staying in bunk beds in a lodge that was heated by a fireplace. The one time I had done that, I got the flu while at camp and had a pretty miserable trip. I was not a seasoned camper when this trip started. I was not looking forward to the **camping** but figured that somehow I could tough this out. I was looking forward to getting to the woods and seeing all the legendary places that had been immortalized in the family deer hunting stories.

We had breakfast in Escanaba and headed for the woods. Of course we had to stop in Ralph and pick up a few supplies at Palluconi's General Store (or whatever it was called that year). That became a ritual. I am not sure we ever needed anything we bought there, but we always bought a sack full of supplies and filled the truck with gas. We took a county road out to a logging road that crossed the Ford River and ended in a swamp. That road was to become the trail to many outdoor adventures over the next decade. As we drove in, my excitement rose. Stan described the places that we passed as we went along.

"There is the road to Uncle Bob's cabin," he gestured as we passed a trail to the right.

"This is the spring where George Brown used to go to get water," he shared as the road dipped through a low spot that was filled with cedars and other trees that don't mind wet feet.

"This is the Taylors' cabin," he said as we passed a gray, weathered structure set back in the trees a few yards. I wondered if the place was haunted. The stories about that place include the death of an inhabitant who apparently died many decades ago when a young member of the hunting party fired a deer rifle past the head of one of his elders as a grouse flushed. The assumption was that the concussion killed the old guy.

Most of the area along the road was vegetated with balsam. It had a green, thickly covered look to it. As we passed Taylor's, the green gave way to a birch ridge to the east. Just past the ridge, there was an opening that Stan called the "Burned Car Draw," so named for the remains of an old car that met its demise during deer season back in the forties. Did you ever notice how people who recreate outdoors give place names to locations based on things that have meaning only to their group? The Burned Car Draw means the same thing to everyone who has ever hunted with us in the Upper Peninsula. The skeleton of the burned car was still there then. It disappeared over the next decade or so.

We backed the truck into a little opening in the trees just north and west of the draw. According to Stan, the family had had a camp in that spot in the past. There was snow everywhere. Big snow. Did I mention that we were planning to **camp**? We set our lawn chairs up in the snow. We stacked our kitchen equipment out in the snow. As Stan constructed a latrine in the snow in a clump of trees behind camp, the realization set in that we were in fact going to **camp**. "I can do this. I can do this. How am I going to do this?" I thought, beginning to panic.

Once we had our camp in order, we got our hunting clothes on and headed out to hunt. In those days, there were no hunting clothes for women. Stan, bless his heart, knew how much I hated to be cold, so he bought me a goose down, blaze orange, one-piece hunting suit, a pair of pac boots, and everything he thought I needed to stay warm.

You should have seen me in that blaze orange suit. Goose down is not Thinsulate. Quite the opposite. In fact you might even call it fatsulate. In those coveralls, with my ammunition belt, sidearm, hunting knife, and rifle, I looked like a cross between Pancho Villa and the Great Pumpkin. My self image in that outfit was really low, and probably so was my mirror image!

In the late afternoon, Stan picked a spot for me to sit. At this point in my outdoor career, I could read which direction was north from a compass but really did not know how to get around or what might constitute a good place to watch. The spot where I spent the next few hours overlooked an opening. I sat alone on a ridge, concealed by a large spruce tree, while Stan went to sit out the afternoon in another location. Those hours were the first time I had ever been alone in the woods. I liked the experience.

The opening in front of me was snow covered. Patches of taller grasses stuck out of the snow here and there. The opening was dotted with chokecherry trees, the tops of which had been broken down by bears. I thought about those bears as it began to get dark, and I wondered if they were still up and around.

On the afternoon set, as I like to call it, you really get a chance to take in your surroundings. I enjoy the anticipation, the chance that you might see the quarry that you are after or that you might see some other unique show of wildlife. There is always something to soak up. You begin to learn what sounds and sights to expect and when to expect them. Where we hunted in the Upper Peninsula, there was always a plane that flew over about 4:10 P.M. Late in the afternoon, you would hear the lonely, cold call of the ravens. Near to dark, there would be the last twitterings of chickadees and nuthatches. If you sat until sunset, you would hear the coyotes begin their mournful yipping north of the "Big Swamp," a huge black spruce swamp where the logging road dead-ended.

After dark, Stan came by to pick me up for the short trip back to camp. Then it was time to start supper. I confess I do not remember anything about supper that night. We must have cooked it in the snow and ate it in the snow. Skipper must have been there, running around camp in the red dickie that we put on him to keep him from getting shot should he wander off. I am sure I made at least two final trips to the privy before Stan closed us in the back of the pickup for the night. It was probably all of 6:30 P.M. by this time.

That is when the realization really hit me that we were actually going to sleep in the back of the truck. We climbed up in the bunk in the front of the box. It was cozy enough. We had our pads and goose down bags. Even had pillows. I snuggled in and tried to get comfortable. Immediately, I began worrying about all the commotion it would cause if I had to get up and go to the bathroom. What bathroom? I tried not to think of it, but immediately I had to go! I tried to ignore it. Finally, I realized that I might as well get up and get it over with. I had to disturb Stan, put my boots on, open the tailgate, and trudge out through the snow. The dog thought it was great fun.

Back in the truck, I climbed into the sleeping bag and hoped to finally settle in. I could not relax. I began to fear that I would suffocate in the back of the truck, die in the night, and be forever cold there in the north woods. I cranked open the window and pressed my face up against it to insure that I would have sufficient oxygen to make it to morning. Stan was sleeping peacefully by that time.

The rest of what happened for the next few days is something of a blur. I imagine that we hunted the next day or so. I think it snowed every day. The snow in the kitchen and around the privy got deeper and deeper. My big boots and my oversized orange suit became harder and harder to drag through the snow. One night when we returned to camp to start supper, Stan fired up the Coleman stove. I should say Stan tried to fire up the Coleman stove. He could not get it to start. He is a very handy guy and there is almost nothing he can't fix, but that stove got the best of him that night. It ended with Stan swearing at the stove, throwing it at a tree, and taking me to dinner at the Dickinson Hotel in Iron Mountain.

At some point, I became so exhausted from staying up all night worrying about breathing and needing to make a nature call that I just became catatonic. I sat in my lawn chair in the snow and said nothing. We were not having fun yet! I would probably never have gone deer hunting again had Stan not recognized the fact that it did not have to be this way. He loaded me in the truck and drove to Norway Lake, where Garrett and Bubbles MacPeake ran a string of cabins called Sportsmen's Paradise. He rented me a cabin and I was the happiest woman in the whole world. I loved the hunting as long as I could sleep in something besides that coffin on the back of the truck (and being able to take a shower did not hurt either).

A few years later, we tried truck camping one more time, on a trip to Yellowstone Park. I had the same experience. After that I decided that I must not like camping, so we didn't do it again. When our daughter Shannon was younger, her friend Mollie Sprouse and her parents, who are campers, got to jabbing me about not being a camper—outdoorswoman that I was supposed to be and all. So, I agreed to go on a joint family camping trip. It was then that I discovered that I don't hate camping. I hate camping in the back of the truck. It was the closed-in feeling, not the overall situation. Tents are fine. There is plenty of air and plenty of space for your head. I would even say that I enjoy it. Sometimes you just need to identify the real problem so you can come up with a solution.

Getting back to the story of the deer hunt, we continued to use the kitchen area from our original camp for lunches. The other hunting camps in the area, which all had cabins or elaborate wall tent set-ups, laughed at us sitting in our lawn chairs eating lunch in the snow. They called us the "open-air camp."

We saw six deer that season. I learned a great deal about myself, and even though I had mistakenly decided that I must not be a camper, I became hooked on hunting. I learned that you don't have to be super-woman to enjoy the outdoors. Take it at your own level. Enjoy what you enjoy and avoid what you don't like.

After Stan called home to tell his folks where we were staying, his dad asked his sister, Sandra, how she thought I got Stan to move into a cabin. She told him, "Why that's easy enough, she just cut him off."

I laugh at the joke, but of course it's not true. At least I didn't do it on purpose or maliciously. What really happened is a good man was smart enough to realize a good hunting partner is worth cultivating. He cared enough to make sure I was a happy **camper.**

The Big Sniffer

· ·

The second year that we hunted deer, I rented a cabin at Sportsmen's Paradise . . . ahead of time. These cabins were nothing fancy, but they were warm, dry, and comfortable. They were situated on Norway Lake, a body of water of approximately eighty acres, between the towns of Ralph and Felch. Since we were not camping near the Burned Car Draw, we only hunted in that area part of the time. The rest of the time, we explored new areas to hunt, using the cabin as our base of operations.

On one of our scouting missions into a new area, I found a place that I really thought looked like a great place to take up an afternoon set. The area that I planned to watch was a small opening in the forest, that was up on a low ridge. The ridge dropped off into a swamp. The slope to the swamp was a maze of deer trails that crisscrossed between the thickly growing balsam. There were deer tracks everywhere, but the big attraction for me was the bear dung.

In those days you could take a bear on your Michigan firearm deer license. Most people presumed that the bears were pretty well tucked in for the winter by mid-November. But, you never know. Part of the thrill of hunting is not knowing what might happen. The idea that I might see a bear and that I might have a chance of taking one made the hunt more interesting.

The year before, one of the highlights of the hunt had been that one of the hunters who had been hunting in the area where we had camped took a bear out of the Big Swamp. We happened upon his party one afternoon just as they dragged the bear out to the road. The hunter who had shot the bear was a grizzled old guy who wore a red plaid jacket. In fact, the whole crew looked like something out of a 1930s hunting calendar. They all lined up and I took their photograph with the bear. You can't imagine how wild this place seemed to a suburban Detroit native.

There is another reason why I chose to sit where the bears had obviously been. I am afraid of and fascinated by them. Now, this is not the wild-eyed, gut wrenching, get hysterical and scream kind of fear. I reserve that for spiders. This is a mildly irrational, nagging in the back of the mind kind of fear that results from having read a few too many bear stories. There is just something about an animal that could eat me that adds a little bit of a thrill to the situation. Choosing to sit in a location where I might see one always seems like a good idea about 2 P.M. As the sun begins to sag on the southwest horizon, the merit of the idea degenerates. This is as close to bungee jumping as I am ever likely to get.

That particular afternoon was cold and gray, but there wasn't any snow on the ground. I scouted the edge of the ridge and chose a clump of balsam at the crest of the slope. The trees were relatively young and only about ten feet tall, with many low branches that would provide good cover. There was a large, craggy stump in the middle of the trees. I thought that would make a good place to sit.

Stan left me in the opening, took the truck, and went to hunt in another location. He told me he would be back at dark to pick me up.

I plunked my "hot seat" down in the center of the charred remains of the tree that was to be my perch for the next few hours and settled in to see what would happen.

Things were pretty quiet all afternoon. As the sun began to set and the temperature began to drop, I heard footsteps in the swamp; a faint crunch of frozen vegetation, an occasional crack of a breaking branch. My heart began to race. The steps came closer, closer. Something was wrong, however. The steps were behind me. I was seated on the stump and could not turn around to look without taking a chance on spooking the critter, whatever it was. The crunching and cracking became progressively louder as the animal approached ever nearer. By now, my heart was beating so loudly that the blood pounding in my ears began to drown out the footsteps.

The crunching stopped but was replaced with a new sound. What was it? I strained my ears to listen, fighting the urge to turn around and look. This might be the buck of the century, and I sure didn't want to ruin my chances. I summoned up all of my self-control and was able to calm my excitement enough to really listen to this new sound. It was sniffing. The animal was standing directly behind the clump of balsam that concealed me and was sniffing. "Sniff! Sniff! Sniff!"

"Do deer sniff?" I wondered ignorantly. "Or is this the bear that I am now hoping not to see in the gathering twilight?"

The animal stopped sniffing but did not leave. It was a standoff. I sat as still as I could. It did not move either. The time ticked away and the light began to disappear.

"Oh, please go away," I implored silently as the darkness began to close in around me.

I knew it would be a long time before Stan came to pick me up. His idea of dark and my idea of dark were not at all the same. It seems the sun always sets earlier wherever I am sitting. Besides, he was not even in the same vicinity, having driven to another area to hunt.

The darker it became, the more frightened I became. By now I was thoroughly convinced that the owner of the bear dung that I had seen earlier was standing behind me trying to decide whether or not I smelled good enough to eat. I became more and more agitated.

"I have had enough of this," I decided. "I'm getting the hell out of here."

At that moment I stood up to leave. The animal that had been standing behind me startled and ran right past me, causing the balsam branches to brush my hunting coat rather violently. I screamed in terror, too shaken to even see what it was. I decided that I was not in control enough to be carrying a loaded rifle, so I unloaded it, lest I shoot Stan.

"Better to be eaten by the beast from the swamp than to shoot my husband," I reasoned.

I walked to the road and arrived there about the time Stan pulled up in the pickup. I was crying hysterically when he got out of the truck. We spent the next few minutes with me wailing uncontrollably while trying to explain what had happened. Poor Stan tried valiantly to analyze the situation and find some rational explanation for my distress. Just as I was beginning to calm, I heard something running toward us. It came faster, faster . . . closer, closer, and as it brushed past my leg I shrieked, "Oh my God, here it comes again!"

That's when Stan must have thought I had lost it altogether, because Skipper, who had jumped out of the truck when Stan pulled up, was now charging past us to get back into the truck. I had not even realized the dog was there and thought he was the Big Sniffer I had encountered earlier.

In the safe light of the next afternoon, I decided that I was not going to let this thing get the best of me. I decided to go back to the same spot to see whether the animal would come back. This time, however, I was going to be smarter. I would not sit on the stump, but would stand in the clump of balsam so I could be more mobile. I took along a few apples and pitched them out in front of my stand in the hope that the apples would entice the animal out into the open so I could see it.

It was a cold, still, gray afternoon. As the light began to fade, the footsteps in the swamp began again. My heart raced as it had the day before. It was *deja vu*. This time, however, the footsteps skirted the clump of trees that provided my cover. Out into the opening walked a little button buck. He was adorable. He had little fuzzy protrusions on his skull where next year's antlers would be. Those little knobs that looked like buttons gave him an almost comical appearance. I stifled a chuckle as he walked up in front of me and began munching the apples that I had tossed out. I could hear the crunch of the apples between his molars and could see the bits of apple falling out of his mouth on either side.

The gray afternoon light became further diffused by huge, soft snowflakes that drifted toward the earth. When the Big Sniffer finished his unexpected snack, he ambled off through the trees and I walked light-heartedly toward the road, full of the delight of the experience.

The Aqua Velva Man

I shot my first buck in 1976 on the opening day of the Michigan rifle season. It is one of my most memorable days in the field, but bagging that first whitetail turned out to be only part of it.

We were staying at Sportsmen's Paradise for the third year. The proprietor, Garrett MacPeake, had taken a liking to us over the years we had stayed with him, so he had fixed up some blinds for us along the edge of a swamp. The three of us planned to go out together opening morning.

Garrett and his wife, Bubbles, were the perfect resort owners. Cordial and friendly, they took a personal interest in us. Garrett, a quick-witted Irishman given to practical jokes, liked my easy smile and exuberant laughter. He nicknamed me "Smiley."

"I'd really like to see Smiley get her first deer," was his excuse for giving me what he considered to be the best place to sit.

We got up well before dawn. As was my habit, I showered, curled my hair, and put on make-up and perfume. Perfume? There are those of you out there right now who are throwing up your hands in disgust. Let me finish the story. You might change your minds.

We warmed up the truck and headed over to pick up Garrett.

When he slid into the front seat next to me, he wrinkled up his nose and looked totally disgusted.

"Good grief, Smiley, how do you ever expect to see a deer when you smell like that," he complained (expletives deleted for a family audience).

"Deer know what you stinky old hunters smell like," I retorted. "They will be curious about me."

He did not look convinced.

We made the ten miles to the trail that led down to our blinds in good time. No other vehicles had driven up the road. We parked at the end of the road and stepped out into the crisp pre-dawn air. It was really COLD.

The snow crunched loudly underfoot as we headed for our stands. Garrett veered off the main trail, as his blind was the first one we came to. My blind was second, and Stan's was the farthest along the edge of the swamp.

I settled in among the dead limbs and brush and waited for it to get light. It was about 6 A.M. when I sat down.

I am a really good sitter. It's the kind of hunting I do best. I rely on my sense of hearing to detect game, and it is hard to hear when you are moving around. I can sit *very* still.

On this particular morning I sat so still and it was so cold that by 9:30 A.M. I had frost on my eyelashes and no sense of feeling in the toes that I hoped were still inside my pac boots. I knew I had to get up and move around before hypothermia set in. I did not want to go back to the truck on my own, because the only way I knew how to get there was to follow the trail we came in on. That trail would go past Garrett, and I did not want to disturb his hunting. Stan isn't all that serious about shooting anything, and he doesn't like to sit anyway, so I knew he would not mind taking me back to the truck by another route. So I walked over to his blind to ask for guide service.

Once back to the truck, I started the engine and took off my boots to warm my nearly frozen toes. Even after the walk back, I was so cold that the tears ran from my cold, watery eyes. Thirty minutes, a cup of coffee, and a candy bar later, I was starting to feel pretty good. So I put my boots back on and decided to take a reconnaissance stroll around the area. I really did not expect to see anything, so I took only my rifle and compass while leaving my hunting knife in the truck. This has turned out to be a rather successful strategy for me, and I have become rather famous for it.

Not wanting to disturb the rest of my party, I crossed the road in the opposite direction from my earlier excursion. It was still very cold, but the sun was out. I followed a fresh deer track. It led to a rather deep depression in the ground. I climbed down into the low spot and sat on a log to rest.

Presently, I heard the not-too-distant sound of crunching snow. It was so loud that I thought that some other hunter had wandered into the area. As the steps approached I realized that it was a deer. My heart pounded wildly. The fact that I was down in the low area effectively camouflaged my presence. As soon as I caught sight of the animal, I clicked off the safety on my Marlin and squeezed the trigger. The animal dropped immediately.

"Are you all right?" a male voice queried.

I did not know what to do. I was so surprised to hear someone speak! As far as I had known, there hadn't been another hunter around for miles. Then I realized that this might not be a good situation. My party did not know where I was. I was alone out there. What if this guy did not have my best interest in mind?

"Get hold of yourself," I reasoned. "Rapists probably do not look for victims in the remote woods of the Upper Peninsula during deer season. Besides, you are not exactly defenseless standing here with that Marlin loaded with 200-grain round noses."

"Yes, I'm all right," I said aloud. "I shot a deer."

"Hey, great. Congratulations," enthused the stranger as he walked over to take a look. "Nice deer!" It was just like all those Saturday morning television shows where they only say three things, depending on which show you watch. It is either "Nice deer, Joe"; "Nice turkey, Joe"; or "Nice fish, Joe." Of course to get it right you have to drawl a little, as in "Neyes feeish, Joe."

"Well, I do have one little problem," I said, using my best damsel-in-distress tone. "I seem to have left my hunting knife in the truck. I wonder if I could borrow yours." (I was hoping against hope that he would not loan it to me.)

"Hey, no problem, but you don't want to do this." (Boy did he have that right!) "I'll get my buddies and we'll take care of this for you," my new acquaintance offered helpfully.

So, he went to get his two friends. They field-dressed the deer, dragged it out of the woods, and loaded it on the truck. I carried the rifles for whoever was dragging. I thanked them profusely and asked the location of their camp so I could drop off a few cases of beer later on. They went on their way and I was sitting there in the truck warming up when Garrett and Stan came out of the woods.

"What kept you guys?" I queried. "It's lunchtime and I am hungry."

Garrett walked around the truck three times, shaking his head in disbelief.

"Well, Smiley," he said finally. "I can believe that you shot it. I can believe that you gutted it. I can even believe that you dragged it to the road. But how the heck did you get it loaded onto the top of the truck?"

I howled with laughter as I retold the events of the morning.

But the day was not over yet! The day had been cold and the low arc of the late November sun had warmed it but little. That evening we returned to the swamp that we had watched in the morning. This time Garrett took the best blind, as I had already had my opportunity. As I stood silently contemplating the edge of a cedar wetland that we referred to as the "Little Green Swamp," I was more aware of the cooling of the air than of the decreasing daylight as sunset approached.

Presently, I heard footsteps. Slowly, I turned my head in the direction of the sounds. Eyes strained, ears strained, pulse quickened. A graceful brown figure made its way toward me. Closer, closer. My ground blind concealed me effectively. I raised my rifle. Closer . . . a doe. I relaxed and lowered my rifle. She approached within five yards. If she realized I was there, she never let on. After a few moments, she made her way east along the edge of the swamp.

Ten minutes passed. The light faded a little, the temperature dropped, and the chickadees made their last little flutterings before nightfall. I thought I heard more footsteps. Again, I slowly turned my head toward the west as my pulse quickened. The footsteps were more deliberate this time. As a deer approached, I could see antlers. I raised my rifle. My heart beat harder. He was a very large, perfect eight-point. Should I? I had taken a nine earlier in the day. Was this greed? I could use someone else's tag. I lowered my rifle and relaxed.

The buck came closer . . . very close . . . a barrel length away. He raised his head from the doe trail and we stood face to face. For some reason, what I remember most vividly was that I could even see his eyelashes. Not in total, but each individual, graceful lash. He stood staring at me; I swallowed nervously. At each swallow, he twitched his ears.

Suddenly I became aware that I might be in danger. I was standing within three feet of a very large buck in the gathering twilight. What if another hunter should see him but not see me? I hadn't known that the hunters who helped me in the morning had even been around. I decided to try to scare him off without disturbing the tranquility of the evening.

"Psst! Psst!" I hissed softly at him. He cocked his head from side to side. I almost laughed out loud at the ludicrousness of the situation. In his own good time, he lost interest in me, put his head down, and followed the doe to the east. I did not see him again.

When we met back at the truck after dark, I could not wait to tell Garrett and Stan about the close encounter. Garrett was pretty disgusted with me. He was one of those meat-in-the-freezer kind of guys. He thought I should have shot that deer so he could tag it.

Even though Garrett did not agree with my strict interpretation of the hunting regulations, he must have decided that some of my deer hunting advice was worth following. The next morning when he climbed into the truck to head for the woods, he was wearing so much Aqua Velva that I could hardly stand to sit next to him.

The Field Ranch
. . . .

In 1977, we made a move that changed the whole course of our lives. We moved to the Field Ranch in Hancock, Wisconsin, where Stan was to be the resident manager. I took the opportunity to return to school and work on a master's degree in Water Resources at the College of Natural Resources in Stevens Point. Living at the Field Ranch was an incredible opportunity. Located in Adams County, one of the famed Sand counties, the ranch was over three thousand contiguous acres; huge by Wisconsin standards. It was a cattle ranch that had changed ownership and was in transformation to a vegetable farm. The ranch buildings were located in the center of the farm, at the end of a dead-end mile-long road. The nearest neighbor was a mile away.

We were to live in the ranch house, one of four residences in the complex. The buildings also included an old block machine shed, a red wood-granary, a steel hay shed, and a quarter-mile-long cattle barn. The outbuildings were connected with amazingly sturdy corrals which were constructed out of massive white pine planks and railroad ties. The first time I saw the ranch, during that summer of 1977, the 1,400 acres under tillage were all planted to sunflowers, and they were in full bloom. It was quite a sight, and so alien to me that I felt like I was on another planet. Apart from the sunflowers, however, I thought the whole area was one of the ugliest places I had ever seen. It was flat. I mean really flat. The parched sand yielded only the scrubbiest of trees. The buildings seemed to stick out of the landscape instead of blending in with it. I was pretty depressed at the thought of living there.

It did not take many weeks, however, before the Field Ranch captured my heart in a way that no other place ever has. Maybe some of it was timing. We had been married almost five years. We had no children at that point, just Skipper. I returned to the flexible time schedule of being a student. Stan became very active in his work, not just managing the Field Ranch, but also farms all over the country. What I am trying to say is that I had time. I certainly had space as well.

The west five hundred acres of the farm were wooded. They were covered in jack pine and scrub oak. There were aspens and marshy areas. The farm was traversed by a network of drainage ditches that provided interesting habitats as well. I learned a tremendous amount in those days about farming, about rural communities, about business, about wildlife, about soils, and about me.

This was a golden opportunity, a chance to live close to the land in a way that most people never will. I took advantage of it.

I bought a bow and learned to shoot it. Stan gave me a muzzleloader. We built a shooting range in the backyard and set up a reloading bench in the basement. Our friends Jim and Elaine Kalmbacher and Dick Stephens were shooters. The five of us spent many pleasant Sunday afternoons at the shooting bench, testing new loads and trying out each other's "iron."

I raised horses in those days. Talk about horse heaven! I could ride for miles with Skipper trotting alongside. I spent many hours doing just that.

The wildlife was incredible. There were hundreds of deer. The grouse population was at the top of the cycle. We had Hungarian par-

tridge, coyotes, geese, ducks, raccoons, woodcock, owls, and many, many other species.

The centerpiece of the Field Ranch wildlife, however, was the sandhill crane. I had never seen one before we moved to the ranch. When we first arrived, in early fall, we would see an occasional nesting pair with their dumpy-looking adolescent youngsters. The very large, long-legged birds looked like something prehistoric, not quite belonging to this era. As fall progressed, the numbers increased, since the ranch is a flocking place for cranes. The numbers grew steadily as the day length decreased. Late in October, for some reason, the whole flock knew that it was time to depart for a friendlier climate. Hundreds, maybe thousands, of birds took to the air in a whir of wings amid the sound of calls that were vaguely but not quite goose-like. The flock circled ever higher in the sky, with the sounds growing ever more faint with increasing altitude. Eventually the multitude of birds appeared as a pinprick in the distance and the sound was carried away from the earth on some distant wind current, not to be heard again until the following spring.

Bowhunting was my excuse to soak up the Field Ranch wildlife show. I would put on my camo coveralls and make-up and head for the woods. The show was never the same. Some evenings the stars of the show would be deer, some close enough to touch with the tip of my broadhead. Truth be known, I never even drew on one. I just did not think I was a good enough shot. (Years later, I took some lessons and made some minor adjustments to my equipment that have changed my attitude in that area.)

One night I had two barred owls calling in the area that I sat in. One glided silently in my direction, lit in the tree above my head, and sat there till I left at dark. Another evening, I sat at the edge of a cornfield while hundreds of woodcock fluttered past my head. On one evening outing, strange whistling sounds drew me to the edge of a ditch, where I found that the beavers had created a new pond. Wood ducks had discovered the pond and had taken up residence there. It was my first glimpse of those wildly colored beauties.

Before our move to the Field Ranch, I fished and hunted. I certainly appreciated the natural world. My years at the ranch ignited a passion for the resources. My time alone in the field raised my self confidence and increased my knowledge. Now, I do not only fish and hunt. I am an angler, I am a hunter, and I am an environmentalist. When I hear the distant call of a sandhill crane in late October or smell the August aroma of sweet fern, my heart drifts back to the Field Ranch, and I am thankful for the chance I had.

Skunked

· · · · · · · · · · · · · ·

One of the joys of living at the Field Ranch was the neighborhood. There were not many neighbors, and those that were there were not close by. There is something about not living too close together that makes for better neighbor relationships.

Our closest neighbors were Tip and Howard Williams. They were farmers. When Howard wasn't farming, he was fishing, hunting, snowmobiling, or talking about those activities. He was one of those lucky people that always seemed to draw a hard-to-get license and always seemed to get the biggest one of whatever it was he was after. He had a good sense of humor as well, and Howard and I went at it "hammer and tongs." He was always trying to pull something on me and I was always trying to pull something on him. Tip threw in and helped whoever was plotting the next attack.

An example of the skulduggery that we pulled might be what I refer to as "The Great Undershorts Caper." One weekend that Tip and Howard went up north snowmobiling with us, we ended up getting our laundry bags mixed up. Not wanting to miss a golden opportunity like that, I washed their laundry and sewed up the flies on all of Howard's jockey shorts. As I recall, a mutual friend of ours, Peggy

Straight, was in on this prank as well. We let Tip in on this and she placed the shorts strategically on top of the stack in Howard's drawer. He put those shorts on one morning when they were headed up north for a bowling tournament. When they arrived after a long drive, Howard made a beeline for the urinal, only to end up standing there in a panic, thinking he had put his shorts on backwards. Those are the kinds of things we did to each other.

One fall we started having trouble with skunks at the ranch. It began with an infestation of grubs in the lawn. The grubs would eat the roots of the grass and the skunks would come in at night and eat the grubs, leaving divots all over the lawn. I am mostly a believer in live and let live, unless I am planning to eat or wear whatever I kill, or unless a critter is trying to move into my house. The skunks were a problem I could not tolerate, however. It wasn't the lawn that put me over the edge. It was the dog. We would let Skipper out in the morning and he would go after the skunks. This resulted in a great deal of extra work (to say nothing of the grocery bill for tomato juice). After that happened the second time, I declared war on the skunks.

One morning I got out of bed and headed into the shower. When I came out of the bathroom, wrapped in a towel, I happened to see a skunk in the front yard under the yard light. I dropped the towel and headed for the gun cabinet. Stan had a nice little Browning .22 semi-automatic with a scope on it. I loaded the rifle and headed out on the front porch. Then I could see that there were two skunks. Someone had told me that if you shoot them in the head, they won't stink. So I stepped stark naked out onto the sidewalk, shouldered the rifle, put the crosshairs on the head of the first skunk, and squeezed off. I must have been quite a sight!

The skunk died instantly, but the advice I was given about shooting them in the head so they don't smell . . . is not correct. I pulled up on the second skunk and dispatched it with equal efficiency and equal olfactory effect. Not exactly dressed for a skunk funeral, I left the beasts for Stan to deal with.

Now Howard had recently returned from an elk hunt and of course had bagged a really fine specimen. All of us were happy for him for his success. He was not satisfied with local admiration, however, and had called the newspaper and had his picture taken and the particulars printed. We were really frosted by that. So that morning when I headed off to work I happened to see Terry, one of Howard's employees, coming up the road in his pickup. I pulled up next to him and rolled down my window.

"Tell Howard he isn't the only great hunter on this road. He should have been looking out the window this morning when I stepped out in the front yard, in the buff, and dispatched two skunks with a .22. It was some pretty fancy shooting all the way around," I bragged as Howard-like as I could.

Frankly, I forgot about the entire incident by the time I arrived home that afternoon. I went about the business of making supper, and just as we sat down to eat, the doorbell rang. Stan went to answer it and called me to the door. There on the front step was a middle-aged woman with a camera hanging around her neck.

"Hello. I'm Adeline Radke from the *Oshkosh Northwestern*. I understand that you are a hunter and that you recently took some nice trophies. I'm here to take your picture and do a story," she said enthusiastically.

"Oh, my God," I gasped, mortified at the situation. "Oh, I am sorry that you went to all this trouble, but I . . . I . . . well, actually, I only shot two skunks," I stammered.

"Well, could I take your picture with them?" Adeline offered, undaunted by the whole situation.

"I buried them in the garden this morning, but I could dig them back up," Stan offered a little too helpfully.

That is when it occurred to me that Howard might have something to do with this. Later, I found out that Adeline was indeed a correspondent for the *Oshkosh Northwestern*. She also bowled on a team sponsored by Howard.

The Bear Hunter

. . . .

One fall Howard asked if Stan and I would like to accompany him and his brother-in-law, Joe Steiner, on a bear hunt. Before Stan could even answer and before we had any of the details of the situation, I answered, "Yes!"

The details turned out to be that Howard would hire some guy up in Ashland to set four bait stations. We would drive up when the season started and would each sit in a tree. If a bear came along, we would have an opportunity to shoot it. This would cost us $200 each. I wasn't sure how I felt about baiting. I had been known to toss out an apple or two when on a deer set, but I had never hunted anything that had been actively baited. But I had committed us, so we headed up to Ashland in mid-September to hunt bear.

I had never seen a tree stand before, let alone used one. The type that we had were the kind that you stand on, putting your feet under two pieces of heavy elastic and using your arms to pull yourself up the tree. When your weight is on the stand, it holds tight to the tree. When you take your weight off of the stand, so that the stand is suspended from your feet by the elastic, you can inch the stand up or down. There were no safety straps, and I had received no instruction on safe gun handling in conjunction with the use of tree stands. Phil Zipp, the Wisconsin Hunter Education Instructor with whom I recently took my instructor apprenticeship, would not have been impressed with this situation.

We began our hunt in the mid-afternoon on a Saturday. We all loaded into Howard's Suburban and stopped first at my bait station so that the guys could help me get up in the tree.

The tree that looked to be situated in the best spot was one that was about 25 yards from the bait. There was a small crotch in the tree about five feet off the ground. We clamped the climber on above that crotch and Stan gave me a boost up onto the climber since it was too high for me to reach by stepping. I believe I mentioned in an earlier chapter that I am something of a chicken when it comes to high places. What I failed to mention is that I am scared to death, even of stepladders. This tree climber was terrifying. As I edged ever farther up the tree, I was sure that death was imminent. I kept thinking that I was high enough, and Howard kept telling me that I needed to get up higher. Finally, when it seemed that I could go no farther, I turned around and insisted that this was it. The fellas said they would be back after dark and headed back toward the road. I heard the Suburban drive off.

I have probably never spent a more boring evening in the woods. There I was, perched on a piece of plywood probably only fifteen feet (my husband says eight, but he can write his own book) or so above a bait pile that consisted of old bread and some anise-smelling substance. I stared at that old bread for three or four hours. The mosquitoes buzzed around. Three raccoons came in to munch on the bread just before dark. That was it. You could not walk around and see the area. You just had to sit there and hope that some poor bear would be overpowered by his love of glorified garbage and would amble in to his demise.

Howard, who was always luckier than he probably deserved to be, shot a 450-pound boar that evening. It was a really nice bear that eventually made a really nice rug. The meat was good as well. It was the only chance I have ever had to eat bear. Howard was the only one who saw anything.

We had one more evening to hunt. So away we went in Howard's Suburban again. This time Howard was only acting as chauffeur. They again dropped me off first. As I climbed up the tree, the weather began to look threatening. The wind was beginning to pick up and the sun had been obliterated by dark clouds.

"Don't worry. If it starts to storm, I'll be back to get you," Howard said reassuringly as he headed back for the road.

He had not been gone half an hour when the lightning started.

"Oh God," I thought in a panic. "I can't stay in this tree if it is going to lightning, but I am afraid to climb down by myself, so what am I going to do?"

I decided to try to climb down. I hung my rifle on a limb as Howard had instructed me to do if I needed to get out of the tree. I am sure that I did not unload it (I told you Phil Zipp was not going to be impressed). I turned around gingerly on the tree stand and put my arms around the tree and clasped my hands together.

"Here goes," I thought nervously. "How hard can this be?"

I edged my feet under the elastic straps, hugged the tree, and lifted my weight off the stand. The stand slipped off my feet and slid clear down to the crotch. There I was, in the middle of one of my worst nightmares. I was hanging from the tree by my arms about ten feet above the tree stand, which was several feet above the ground. There was nothing to do but to slide down the tree and hope I could hang on. I loosened my grip on the tree while still trying to keep my hands clasped together. As I slid, I picked up momentum. When I reached the tree stand, I was sliding out of control. The stand broke my fall, which was the good news. The bad news was that I ended up with my lower legs pinned between the tree stand and the tree, bent at the knees, with the rest of my body hanging head down toward the bear bait.

"What will I do if a bear comes in now?" I thought hysterically. A clear-thinking person would have realized that I had made such a commotion that there was probably not a bear left anywhere in the section.

I thought about taking my hunting knife and cutting off my legs at the knees. It didn't turn out to be that serious. I was able to loosen one of the wing nuts that held the unit together so I could get my legs out. Fortunately, I was not that far off the ground, so the fall did not hurt me, much.

I took a stick and used it to get my rifle down out of the tree, picked up the tree stand, and headed for the road. The trail out to the road was bordered by very tall grasses that were way up over my head. The trail was well worn, both by the guide and by bears. I approached the road but did not stand out in it, since I did not want others to know where the guide was baiting. I just thought that with the lightning and rain, Howard would be back after he picked up the others.

He came back all right, but he never even slowed up on the way by. He did not even look in my direction. I stepped out into the road, waving at the back of a Suburban that was empty, save Howard.

"You S.O.B., Howard," I shouted in anger. Of course, I did not use the initials. I used the real words . . . and then some. "What am I going to do now?" I thought.

About that time, the rain quit and I realized that no one was going to come back to get me until after dark. I did not want to spend the next three hours standing there next to the road. And I did not want to stand in the tall grass, where I couldn't see in any direction. So I decided to walk back into the clearing where the bait was.

I tried to climb back into the tree that I had fallen out of, but the crotch that the tree stand had to go above was too high for me to step up to. I had to find another spot. There was an apple tree nearby. I climbed up into the top of that, without the use of the climber. I had ceased to think of elevation as some sort of advantage over the bear and had begun to think of it as protection from the bear. I knew it would be after dark when my party returned, and I wanted a safe place to sit after the sun went down. I know this is all somewhat irrational, but I was in a fairly irrational state of mind after all that had happened that afternoon.

I was just beginning to feel pretty pleased with the way I had found a nice safe place to settle in, when I noticed that all the apple limbs around me were scarred up. "Those scars are bear claw marks," I thought with dismay. So much for my safe refuge.

I climbed down out of the tree and looked for a tree I could use the tree stand in. I picked a nice straight aspen, fastened the tree stand around it, and shinnied up the tree like I had been doing it all my life. I spent the rest of the uneventful evening staring at that bait pile.

Later that night, Stan and I got to talking about another friend of ours, Bill Soik, who had taken his girlfriend to New Orleans for the weekend to see a boxing match. It was a big one, Sonny Liston or Muhammad Ali (since I am not a boxing fan, I don't remember which it was). It cost them $200 each for the tickets to the fight.

"Can you imagine spending $200 to go watch two guys beat each other up?" I crowed self-righteously.

"Can you imagine spending $200 to go spend a weekend sitting in a tree?" Stan replied with a twinkle in his eye.

The Big Buck

. . . .

The summer of 1980 we did a lot of shooting. We had a rifle range set up in the backyard and a reloading bench in the basement at the ranch.

While doing the laboratory work for my graduate project at the University of Wisconsin-Stevens Point, I met Dick Stephens. He ran the Environmental Task Force Laboratory at the university and actually did much of the chemical analysis for the water pollution project that I was working on. Dick is a gun buff, so it didn't take long for us to strike up a friendship on that basis. He introduced Stan and me to Jim and Elaine Kalmbacher from Fond du Lac. They were shooters and hunters as well. Elaine and I were both "nice Polish girls." Our friendship has been strong and has included many outdoor adventures in the years since.

The five of us would get together to shoot almost every weekend. It became a regular Sunday ritual—out to the range in the afternoon and down to the reloading bench in the evening to tinker up next week's loads. This was serious shooting. Tight groups were the order of the day.

We did have one ritual, however, that was not too serious: the

"Simulated Grizzly Bear Attack." We usually ended our shooting for the day with that event. Since there are very few grizzlies in central Wisconsin, we had to simulate their attack by putting up oversize or over-ripe cabbages, watermelons, or pumpkins on the backstop downrange. This was a handgun, fire-at-will event. No one ever knew who really stopped the bear, but with that much lead flying downrange, the bear never did get us.

One Sunday, we headed up to the Marathon County shooting range to do some handgun shooting. There is a really nice range there that has a pit down under the targets. Each person can go downrange to change or check targets and the rest of the shooters can continue shooting safely.

Elaine and I pulled out our handguns. I don't remember what she was shooting, but I had a Colt Python .357 that Stan had given me a number of years before. I am an excellent rifle shot, but handgunning is a little more challenging.

We started at the one hundred-yard range. That is a really long distance to do any significant handgunning. I remember that there was a man at a neighboring bench who made some snide remarks about our ability to shoot those "hog legs," as he called them.

We loaded up and each took six shots. Then we went down to the pit to check our targets. Stan, Jim, and Dick were already down there checking theirs. When we saw our targets, we couldn't believe it. Each target had six shots in the bull's-eye. I had never had that good of a target even at twenty-five yards. We were really "pumped." We each pulled down our targets to save them, marched back to the shooting bench, plunked the targets where the neighboring shooter could get an eyeful, and commenced shooting again.

We never put another round on the paper that day.

Later that week, at work, Dick let it slip that the holes in our targets exactly matched the diameter of a pen that one of the guys had in his pocket that day. I imagine they had a really good laugh watching Elaine and me strut around with those targets, and an even better laugh when we couldn't duplicate our efforts. This is one of those stories that I think is a lot funnier now, fifteen years later, than I thought it was at the time.

That year we invited Dick to join us and Jim Empson, a friend of ours from Traverse City, Michigan, on our annual whitetail pilgrimage to the Upper Peninsula. As the summer progressed, Dick came along with some reportedly super loads for my .308. I practiced with them and they were good. I was printing targets with a ³/₄-inch group at one hundred yards—some damn fine shooting. I decided to use them for the hunt.

By the time we decided to head for the north woods, Dick was seriously interested in Mary Braatz, a wildlife artist who had been painting a mural in the stairwell of the building where we worked. We invited Mary to go along as well. As usual, we had a cabin at Sportsmen's Paradise.

The second afternoon of the season, we decided to hunt in the vicinity of Burned Car Draw. Stan's family was camping there, so we did not want to disturb them. We opted to head a little north toward the Big Swamp. Stan and I would walk north on the little track that cut the west end of the swamp. Dick, Mary, and Jim would take the rye field on the south side.

On the way into the area, we encountered a pickup and camper stuck in the road. Stan, Dick, and Jim helped the driver extricate himself. In my view all this was eating up valuable hunting time. Not that I wouldn't help, but there is only so much time to find a place to sit for the evening, and the walk through the swamp was a long one. I guess you could say I was impatient.

Finally, mercifully, we were out of the truck and headed north through the black spruce and cedars. At the north end of the road there

was a large opening with a few scattered, large balsam. North of that, the topography rose sharply to a sidehill covered with a thicket of young aspen. Buck rubs lined the edge of the swamp and the edge of the aspens. Stan headed off to the west. He would probably walk most of the time. I looked for a place to sit out the remaining daylight and watch the edge of the swamp.

I couldn't seem to find a good spot. Up on the hill, I didn't have enough cover. Down closer to the swamp, it seemed I couldn't see enough of the area. I moved several times. Finally, about forty-five minutes before dark I decided to sit under a large balsam about seventy-five yards from the edge of the swamp. As I walked up to the tree, I spooked a deer just inside the edge of the swamp. I could hear it breaking ice and snorting as it ran off.

I figured that I had just blown my opportunity, but I settled in under the tree anyway. I didn't have any better idea. About ten minutes later, I began to hear ice breaking far into the swamp. The cracking and crunching got louder and louder, but daylight was beginning to slip away. My heart raced, the blood pounded in my ears. Would the animal come out in the open, and even if it did, would it be before dark? Would it be a buck? All the unanswered questions are what make hunting such an exciting activity.

The crunching and cracking proceeded steadily to the edge of the swamp. Without hesitation a magnificent buck stepped right out in front of me to my left—my best shot. It stood there, quartering slightly toward me. All I could see were antlers. This was no baby, but a fully mature deer, at least 3½ years old.

Calmly, almost eerily calmly, I raised my rifle and squeezed the trigger. No buck fever here. Just all business. The shot rang out and the animal just stood there motionless. I was incredulous. It never occurred to me that I could have missed. I did not fire a second shot. I just stood up, shocked.

As soon as I stood, the buck bolted into the swamp. I couldn't believe it.

Stan had always told me to remember two things when you shoot an animal. Remember where it was when you shot it, and remember where it was when you last saw it. I wouldn't need to worry about forgetting either. That scene is etched indelibly in my memory.

I walked directly to the spot where I shot the buck. There were big sprays of bright red blood all around. A lung shot, I thought hopefully. Then my heart sank as I looked at the swamp, the "Big Swamp" in the gathering twilight.

What should I do? There was a pretty clear blood trail—not little drips, but huge sprays. He couldn't go far, but then he might not need to in the black tangle ahead of me.

I decided to get Stan to help me. That has been the great thing about our relationship. I have never had to feel self-conscious about asking for help. Confident and competent, Stan has never been one to belittle my competence when I have asked for assistance. I had one problem, however. I did not know where he was. I hated to break the tranquility of the evening, but I didn't want to lose this deer either. I finally yelled Stan's name as loudly as I could. He came over in a few moments. Having heard me shoot, he had already been on his way.

Together we tracked the animal into the swamp and found him there under a spruce. Stan took out his hunting knife and knelt down to field-dress the magnificent buck that I was so lucky to get. Before he inserted the blade of his knife, he straightened up, leaned over toward me, and with a twinkle in his eye asked, "Did you see if you could get any other guys to do this for you?"

Do It in the SNOW!

· ·

"So, did you ever do it on the back of a snowmobile?" asked a rather famous executive of an outdoor-related organization over after-dinner drinks with a small group in a big-city hotel. The executive shall remain nameless for the purpose of this narrative. I howled with laughter (something I am famous for) but left them wondering. I'll leave the reader wondering as well, but the question raised the memory of another snowmobile incident.

It was Valentine's weekend in 1981. Stan and I decided to haul our sleds to the Upper Peninsula of Michigan. We rented a cabin in Iron Mountain and arrived late on Friday night. We dropped our gear and headed back across the Wisconsin state line to Spread Eagle and a little supper club called the Eagle's Nest. In those days, they made a pretty mean Bloody Mary and an even meaner steak. I had one of each.

Saturday morning we packed some snacks and headed for the woods. Our plan was to snowmobile in the area where we generally hunted. We had never done that and thought it would be fun to see the area in winter. We drove the Jeep down a sparsely used road and parked off the roadway in a plowed-out area that led to a cabin. The area was deserted.

After dropping the sleds, we suited up and headed up the logging road toward Burned Car Draw. The road was unplowed. A cabin on the creek about a quarter mile up the road created enough traffic so the trail was packed that far. Beyond that the snow was deep and unbroken.

Stan broke trail. His sled was larger and more powerful (does this surprise anyone?). Mine had a smaller "footprint," which means that the track was narrower and the sled more likely to get stuck. I had to stay in Stan's track to stay on top of the snow. "You'll be OK as long as you keep your speed up," he told me after extricating my sled from the deep snow for the third time. This is an inside joke with us from our farming days. When your speed is no longer "up," you are stuck.

The scenery was wonderful. The sky was a clear, bright blue, the mid-morning sun sparkled diamond-like on the snow. The track of a single deer crossed our trail just as we reached Burned Car Draw. That solitary track made me feel lonely.

We were destination snowmobilers. Most of our time on sleds was spent in reaching a destination. The destination that day was a lunch spot over on Silver Lake. It was a pretty good run considering the number of times we got stuck. Did you ever notice how outdoor activities seem to be a good excuse for eating? The cafe at Silver Lake is what our outdoor crew refers to as a good pie stop. As few and far between as pie stops are in most of the areas we recreate in, almost any place that serves pie is a good pie stop. Of course, you cannot have pie without chili and burgers first. So that is what we did.

The run back to the truck in the afternoon was easy sledding. We ran on our old track and the bright, sunny afternoon settled the snow. A mile or so before we arrived at the Jeep, we decided to get off the track and play in the unpacked snow. We both promptly got stuck. Getting unstuck required a good deal of effort and we got pretty well sweated up inside our snowmobile suits. So, when we arrived at our vehicle, hot, sweaty, tired, and thirsty, we took off our suits (actually I think we stripped to our long underwear), took some sodas (I think they were sodas) from the cooler, got out some cheese and crackers, and sat there on a warm winter afternoon in the secluded north woods, enjoying a picnic. Well, there we were in our underwear in the secluded north woods and, well . . . you know . . . one thing sort of led to another.

In the end we must have fallen asleep in the back of the Jeep because next thing we knew there was a roar of snowmobile engines. I peered out the window (keeping a low, covered profile), only to find that we were completely surrounded by trucks, trailers, and snowmobilers who were getting ready to go "do it in the snow."

Winter Celebration

· ·

Many communities in Wisconsin celebrate annual events in some way. Almond has its "Tater Toot," Hancock has a Labor Day "Chicken Barbecue," and Plainfield celebrates "Bean Fest." Every winter, Fond du Lac, the community on the southern tip of Lake Winnebago, has "Winter Celebration." Back in the early 1980s, Jim and Elaine Kalmbacher lived in a house that had canal access to the lake. One year they invited us to come over for the winter festivities.

We got out of bed on Saturday morning with the idea of driving over. While preparing to depart, I said, "Why don't we snowmobile over?"

Never one to hang back on an opportunity to snowmobile, Stan agreed. So I put a change of underwear, make-up, and my curling iron (hey, you need to assess priorities!) in a ziploc bag and stowed them in the trunk of my sled.

We were not sure whether we could find the trails that would take us where we wanted to go, but we headed southeast toward Fond du Lac.

"We'll just go east when we can and south when we have to," Stan advised. "When we get to Lake Winnebago, we'll take a right!"

By automobile, the trip would have been about seventy miles. It must have been over two hundred miles on the trails, because it took all day. We left the ranch about 10 A.M. The day was bright, sunny, and not too cold, only about zero. We knew that we could follow the trail system as far as Wautoma. When we reached that area, we were able to obtain a trail map that would take us as far as Berlin.

The trails were washboard rough. When the snow is old and the trail groomers haven't been through recently, the snow freezes into ridges and valleys. The uneven terrain pounds your posterior and vertebrae as you ride. My sled did not have as comfortable a suspension as Stan's, so he traded with me occasionally to afford some relief.

In Berlin, we stopped at a snowmobile dealer for oil to mix with our fuel. We bought enough for the return trip and hid it in his yard. We also had lunch and obtained further trail directions for the trip from Berlin to Fond du Lac.

The balance of the trip was grueling. I was tired. I was cold. My hands ached from holding the throttle in. My back ached. Each mogul in the trail pounded my already bruised bottom. I could not wait to get there. It was well after dark when we knocked on the Kalmbacher's back door. As Elaine opened it, I chirped, "I sure hope it is Miller time."

"It is," she said. "That's the good news. The bad news is it's your night to cook."

Sunday did not turn out to be a very good day for a Winter Celebration. A late winter blizzard had set in and there was a whiteout on Lake Winnebago. After a hearty breakfast, we decided to fuel up and head for home. Out on the lake the wind was fierce. It forced its way in around the edges of my face mask, stinging as it carried the pelting snow into contact with my skin. We couldn't see anything, so we hugged the shoreline as we crept along, looking for the trail we would need to take off the lake.

"Why do I get myself into these situations?" I thought disgustedly.

Clearly, this had been all my idea.

Once we left the lake, the wind and blowing snow subsided enough so we could see where we were going. After we crossed the last major road we would need to cross, we abandoned the snowmobile trails and took to the county roads. We did not need to worry about traffic, because the roads were drifted to an impassable level. Since it was still snowing, and Sunday besides, the county road crews were not working.

We detoured into Berlin to refuel and then went on to Wautoma. The roads were quite a bit smoother and faster going than the trails had been the day before. We arrived in Wautoma at dark and stopped at the Silvercryst Supper Club for dinner. It felt good to take off our bulky snowmobile suits and heavy helmets and stretch out. We had a table near the fireplace. As we ate dinner, only sixteen miles from home, we talked pretty smartly about our adventure/ordeal of the preceding days.

We were feeling pretty smug about ourselves by the time we headed for the coat room to suit up for the trip back to the ranch. Our smugness did not last long. In the coat room, a group of people were just coming in for dinner. They had snowmobiled from Copper Harbor, Michigan, that day.

On the way back to the ranch, we stopped at Tip and Howard's to brag about our weekend exploits. Tip was off to a bowling tournament, but we visited with Howard for a while. Howard poured us each a drink. I had a peppermint schnapps. I am not much of a drinker and never have been. One is about my limit. I certainly do not drink and drive, and I wasn't one to drink and snowmobile either. I confess I did not think one drink would cloud my judgment, and I did not think there was much to worry about with home less than a mile away on a dead-end road.

That one drink must have caused me to feel a bit frisky. When we left Howard's, I ran ahead, jumped on Stan's sled, and challenged him to a race. I rocketed up the road toward the ranch. As I approached the turn into the driveway, I realized that I was going too fast to make the turn safely. If I tried, there was a chance I would roll the sled on the icy road. My alternative was a steep snowbank ahead where the town plow had been piling up snow all winter. I took the snowbank.

As the sled flew up over the edge of the rough, frozen snow, it became airborne. I lost control of the rocket, flew off the back, and hit my head on the frozen snow. The sled flew ahead of me, rolling over several times, breaking the windshield, and cracking the fiberglass hood.

Meanwhile, Stan had tried valiantly to keep up, but the sled he was riding was not nearly as powerful. Just as he saw me fly over the snowplow embankment, the belt broke on the sled he was riding, leaving him stranded by the mailbox.

When I picked myself up out of the snow, I turned to see Stan running toward me.

"I'm all right! I'm all right!" I yelled at him, thinking that he was concerned for my safety.

"My sled! My sled!" he exclaimed in anguish as he ran right by me toward the disabled snowmobile.

Tippy Canoe

· ·

It was one of our closest brushes with divorce: canoeing on the
Plover River.

Neither Stan nor I had ever been in a canoe. Our friends Jim and
Elaine Kalmbacher had just purchased a Mad River Canoe. It was a
pretty high-tech piece of equipment in those days. Its design made it a
good choice for the whitewater canoe school that Elaine had signed
them up for. They thought they would bring their canoe over to Stevens
Point to try before their canoe school vacation. We planned to canoe
with Dick Stephens and his new love at the time, Mary Braatz. Dick
and Mary had both raced canoes before they met each other. They
loaned us Mary's canoe and used Dick's themselves.

We planned to canoe the Plover from Jordan Park down to Iverson
Park. It is a wonderful stretch of river. The shoreline has been pro-
tected from development by a variety of conservation mechanisms.
There is only one place along the run that you can detect any development. The rest of it is relatively wild and natural. I think the trip is
supposed to take about three hours. We planned to stop at the mid-
point and have lunch. It sounded like an idyllic day.

We dropped the canoes at Jordan and shuttled a vehicle to Iverson so we would have transportation at the take-out point. Finally, we had everyone loaded in canoes. Dick and Mary went first, then the Kalmbachers, with Stan and me bringing up the rear. I sat in the back, for some reason that I can't remember.

It was a fiasco. Dick and Mary glided ahead, far ahead. Their canoeing mirrored their brand new personal relationship—smooth as glass. Jim and Elaine had some trouble learning to work with their new canoe. Stan and I struggled far behind. What seemed to me should be just an easy trip down a small river turned out to be a major undertaking. The water was low, so it was slow going. There were hundreds of deadfalls to be worked around.

I had the mistaken idea that we would glide along, paddling a bit to steer, enjoying the wildlife. It was certainly there to enjoy. Around one bend we saw mallards take to the air; around the next, deer were grazing peacefully.

In our canoe, nothing was peaceful. Stan did not view this as an idyllic outing. This was a challenge. We were in a craft doing a skill he

knew nothing about and we were **behind** the other canoes. It was as if his manhood was on the line.

I cannot emphasize enough how compatible we normally are in recreational situations. This was a different story. He kept turning around and trying to tell me what I was doing wrong. Doing wrong? We were headed in the right direction, albeit slowly. And anyway, what did he know about this? He had never done it either.

Lunch was really a quiet affair. Oh, Dick and Mary conversed breezily—the first blush of new love and all. Jim and Elaine were relatively quiet, and Stan and I sat there in icy silence. The level of conversation in each case a direct indication of the successfulness of the teamwork in the canoe.

The second leg of the trip was "trouble in River City." We were both tiring, the snags increased in frequency, and the others were far ahead. Finally, Stan turned around to direct me about what I should be doing just one too many times.

"Why the Hell are you trying to tell me what to do?" I said belligerently. "You don't know anything about this yourself."

I swung my canoe paddle at his head. I didn't hit him, but the momentum of my swing swamped the canoe and we both ended up sitting on the bottom of the Plover River, looking rather ridiculous. You can't imagine how hard it is to regain your decorum and return to some semblance of teamwork with a person that you just tried to bonk with your canoe paddle.

We switched ends of the canoe for the balance of the trip. He did not do any better than I did. He kept steering us toward snags. Each one had a bigger spider on it than the next. As we slid under the snags, those spiders were right next to me. You remember the "wild-eyed, gut-wrenching, get hysterical and scream" kind of fear that I said I reserve for spiders? Well, I got to exercise it that day. I was sure that Stan was steering me into those spiders on purpose.

Mercifully, the day ended at Iverson Park. When we arrived, Dick and Jim had already made a trip to shuttle vehicles. Mary was talking along, trying to make light conversation. Elaine, who had not had much better of a trip than me, said nothing. I ranted and raved about the events of the afternoon.

Finally, Elaine piped up in the direct way that only she can pull off. "I don't know what you are so ornery about," she said. "You didn't just spend $800 for a damn canoe."

That pretty well put things in perspective.

The Cabin
. . . .

Mushroom hunting was always a major May event for us. Stan tried to arrange his planting schedule so that we could meet Pat and Jim Empson in the Upper Peninsula to hunt morels. The elms were in just the right stage of decline in the Ralph area in the late seventies and early eighties, so that morels could be found by the basketful. Some springs we found as many as six bushels of them.

We would cook them up fresh as many ways as you could imagine. We'd saute them in butter, mix them with scrambled eggs, or split them lengthwise, roll them in eggs and cracker crumbs, and fry them like so many pork chops. Whatever we couldn't eat we would freeze and take home.

Mushroom feasts were always well accompanied. Garrett would likely come along with a package of venison steak, or we might catch some trout out of Norway Lake.

There was one thing about mushroom hunting that I didn't like—ticks. The emergence of mushrooms and ticks seemed to be strategically timed to peak in concert. This is probably some quirk of evolution that provides ticks with a reproductive advantage.

I actually encountered my first tick one July while trout fishing on the Ford River. We were staying at Sportsmen's Paradise. Fishing the Ford involves a fair amount of beating down through the brush to get to the water. As I recall, we spent a good deal of time that first day extricating spinnerbaits from alders. When we arrived back at the cabin late in the afternoon, I took off my jeans to find both legs covered with ticks. I shrieked in terror. I've already told you how I feel about spiders. To me, ticks are just glorified spiders. I had hundreds of them on my legs! They would have eaten me alive if Stan had not been there to take them off.

But over the years, I have developed a tolerance for ticks. They have become just something I have to put up with to get morels.

One year we arrived at Sportsmen's Paradise for the annual morel fest and Garrett informed us that he had put the resort up for sale.

"Yep, Smiley," he related. "We're going to retire in the Lower (Peninsula). I am going to sell the lot next to my house. You kids really ought to buy it."

The lot had about 145 feet of frontage on Norway Lake and had a number of really fine red pine trees on it. The view was gorgeous. The lake was about eighty acres, undeveloped on most of the shoreline. There was a no-motor rule, so the peacefulness attracted fishing loons, ospreys, and bald eagles.

This was not Stan's style. He would have preferred a remote acreage. I was a lake woman, however. It seemed perfect to me, close to deer hunting, great fishing, snowmobiling, and bushels of morels. I wanted to build a cabin on it. Since Garrett was willing to sell it on a land contract, we bought it. It was just one of many concessions that Stan has made over the years in the interest of keeping me happy.

That fall when we arrived for deer season, I spent a great deal of time just standing on the lot, imagining what the cabin would be like. I thought about the exact position, what orientation would provide the best view, and which spot would remove the smallest number of those gorgeous red pines.

Stan agreed that we could build the following year. There was one condition. I had to assume the role of general contractor, because he would be too busy farming during the building season to oversee the job. Hey, I could do this. What pipefitter's daughter worth her salt couldn't manage to get a hunting shack constructed in time for deer season?

We spent most of the winter looking at log home plans. We sent for catalogs and visited models. The day we stepped inside a model of a Boyne Falls Log Home in Coon Valley, Wisconsin, I knew that was it. I just felt like I could sit down in that place and never leave. The company has since gone out of business, but they made the most beautiful, hand-peeled, cedar log home kits. We drew up a plan for a very small kit. It had a combined kitchen, dining, living area on the first floor, with a bath and one small bedroom. We planned to use the loft for a bedroom and finish a bedroom in the basement. It had a wide front porch that ran the width of the front of the cabin.

In the spring we got our financing in order, paid off the lot, ordered the kit, hired a contractor to construct the cabin, and waited for August, when the kit would be delivered. That mushroom season, I spent hours standing on the lot, pretending I was sitting in front of my picture window and admiring the lake.

During the summer I made many trips to Ralph. Sometimes I flew up by myself and sometimes Tip drove up with me. I visited the Dickenson County Health and Sanitary Code office for septic and well permits. I visited the Building and Construction Code Commissioner for a building permit. I rode out to the job site with the man from the power company to show him where I wanted the power pole moved. I had picked out a site for the cabin that would require no tree removal. I had to fight with the contractor over that.

"Those trees are going to die anyway," he lectured. "You might as well let us take them out now. You'll see. You will have to pay to take them out later."

I stood my ground.

The basement went in in early August. I went up to see the site when the footings were poured. The builder had oriented the cabin a few feet differently than I had instructed. That meant that we would see a cabin down the lake out of our window, instead of viewing only the undeveloped wetland across the lake. I was disgusted. The fireplace footing was only six feet long. Not knowing anything about construction, I questioned the contractor about whether a twelve-foot fireplace could be built on a six-foot footing.

"That fireplace is too big for the room it is going into," he told me expertly. "The one we poured will work better."

"You bid a twelve-foot fireplace, that is what I want, and that is what you are going to put in," I ordered rather loudly, with just a touch of pipefitter starting to show. I wondered if he would have tried to pull these things on my husband.

A few weeks later $32,000 worth of cedar logs arrived at the construction site. It was the most money I had ever spent in my life. I went up to see the start of the construction. They were the most beautiful color—like gold shimmering in the afternoon sun reflecting off the lake. I could not wait to move in.

About two weeks later I received a call from the contractor.

"The Building and Construction Code Commissioner has shut down the job," he relayed.

"Oh my God," I gasped. "Why?"

"The site you picked is in violation of shoreland zoning."

"Shoreland what?" I inquired ignorantly.

These days I teach courses about zoning. In those days, I was completely ignorant about the subject.

"What should I do?" I asked.

"Better call the County," advised the contractor.

So I called the Building and Construction Code Commissioner to inquire what had happened.

"Well, young lady," he counseled. "It seems that you are in violation of shoreland zoning. Your lot is only ninety-six feet wide on the end where you are putting your cabin, and you need to have one hundred feet."

I had taken my plans in for approval when I got the building permit, so I never dreamed anything like this could happen.

"What happened here is a little bit of local politics," the gentleman from the county related. "It seems that the township supervisor from a neighboring township complained. A few years ago, a tavern in her jurisdiction burned down. Since the property owner could not get a perk test that would allow a conventional septic to be put in, she has a burr under her tail about anyone else that builds. She accused me of trading you the building permit for sexual favors."

Sexual favors? That was it. I was wild. Who was this floozie and what was I going to do to her? I was going to tear her hair out. I was going to. . . .

But what was I going to do about $32,000 of cedar logs sitting on my lot with the rainy season about to start?

"That's no problem," the official told me. "You'll just apply for a variance. There will be a meeting of the Appeals Committee to decide your case. Since the cabin will be situated in the same relation to the lake and road as the one next to it, and since the lot is well above lake level, there should be no problem."

"Should I come for the meeting?" I asked naively.

"No, don't do that. Just let me handle it," he said.

So I figured I didn't have any choice but to trust him. The construction restarted a week later.

Finally, in late October, the cabin was ready to move into. This was the first place I ever owned. I loved hanging the wildlife print drapes on the picture window. I loved hanging the gun rack on the wall by the stairs. I loved putting the afghan over the back of the sofa. I loved putting the dishes and spices in the cupboard.

I loved it when Stan started the first fire in the twelve-foot fieldstone fireplace—not fake stones, but the real thing, split on the inside of the cabin and whole on the outside. The firebox would take a four-foot log. The mantle was a huge red-pine log that the contractor cut on two sides. He left it round on the front and bottom and left the bark on. Once we got into the project, he actually turned out to be a great guy with an appreciation of the beautiful piece of work we were trying to create. Above the mantle, next to the fieldstones, we hung Stan's coyote rug. On the mantle, we placed a gift from the Empsons, a print of a wolf looking over some rocky Upper Peninsula ledge.

We were in. That first evening we watched the sun set in a low late-October arc over the lake. The chickadees and nuthatches had already discovered our bird feeder. The smell of the cedar surrounded me. As I lay in bed in the loft that evening, I thought I must be in heaven and heaven was mine. The firelight danced on the beautiful spruce ceiling boards as I drifted off to sleep.

Changes
. . . .

Just about the time we built the cabin, Stan began growing pota-toes. Now, he was no longer just managing farms for other people, he was doing his own farming. This required a higher degree of financial risk and a higher level of time commitment. Still, we went up to the cabin every chance we could, more in the winter and less during the hectic growing season. Often that meant a late Friday evening depar-ture, a five-hour drive, and a post-midnight arrival.

I soaked up every minute that we were there. Every cup of coffee at the cabin was a special event. Meals cooked there tasted ever so much better. When we left the cabin each time, I would change the sheets on the bed, gather up the used towels, and leave everything picture per-fect for the next arrival. At the ranch, I always had clean linens packed and ready for the next trip north.

I had never intended to have any children. My intention had al-ways been to spend my time pursuing a career. I had been doing just that for ten years. After Stan and I moved to the Field Ranch, I earned a master's degree in water resources from the University of Wisconsin-Stevens Point. When I graduated, the dean of the College of Natural Resources, Dan Trainer, hired me to be his assistant. He was the best "boss" anyone could ever ask for. I was completely happy in my role there. Trainer really likes women, in every positive sense of that statement. He gave me every chance and encouragement to succeed. Working with him, my self-concept rose immeasurably. For the first time in my career, I began to feel comfortable in my own skin.

Dan Trainer is a real hunter, and a successful one, so he often has bounty to share. There was always a great deal of talk about hunting and outdoor activities around our office. Bonnie Clark, who worked with us, had a cabin in northern Wisconsin and spent a good deal of time fishing and deer hunting. It seems that a core of friends who are involved in an activity is an encouragement to stay involved, even if you do not do the activity together. This is probably especially true of hunting. For months ahead of deer season each year, the three of us would spend our coffee breaks and lunches discussing strategies for the hunt and telling the same old stories over and over.

Perhaps it was the "ticking of the biological clock," or perhaps it was maturing into a more confident woman. Whatever it was, in 1982 I changed my mind about starting a family and talked Stan into trying to have a baby. I called it an investment in "grandmotherhood."

Along about October, when we were grading potatoes for storage, Trainer gave me a goose that he had shot on one of his hunting excursions. I had never cooked one before, so I tackled the task with a vengeance. Cranberry stuffing and the "whole nine yards."

It was a Saturday, and I was helping grade potatoes in the shed. I had never done that before. Basically, you stand by a belt, potatoes whiz by, and you pick out the damaged ones and throw them into a heap so they don't rot in the storage bins and spoil the rest. I would grade for a while and then go into the kitchen to check dinner. There were several local women who were grading as well. I was an extra.

It seemed whether I was grading spuds or checking the goose, I was nauseated and dizzy. I couldn't decide if the smell of the cooking goose was doing it, if I was having a bad day, or if I was just a wimp next to the other women. They graded two-handed. It seemed not to bother them at all. I stood there clutching the side of the elevator with one hand to keep from tipping over as the potatoes whirred by. They seemed to float on the belt. My stomach vaulted up and down. First I was hot, then I was dizzy. Man, what must these women think of me? I decided it must be the goose.

"Don't bring me any more of those darn geese," I lectured the dean on Monday. "I haven't felt the same since I started cooking that one on Saturday."

Two weeks later, I went to the dean's office and closed the door. He always knew it was serious when I closed the door.

"I have some good news and I have some bad news," I stated as lightly as possible to avoid crying in an emotional situation. "The good news is that goose did not make me sick. The bad news is that I am likely to be somewhat under the weather for the next few months. The good news is that I am pregnant."

The baby would come in early June, right at the start of summer break for the university. I thought I had everything pretty well figured out.

What I had not figured on was morning sickness that lasted twenty-four hours per day for three months. That really put a crimp on my outdoor activities for the fall. We would drive up to the cabin on Friday nights after potato harvest was over, only to spend the weekend with me too nauseated to do anything.

The opening day of the Wisconsin deer season, I walked to a stand of sunflower stubble out behind the barn. I was too nauseated to get any farther from the house. We were not planning to go to Michigan until Thanksgiving. It was a foggy morning. Before the fog lifted, I saw twenty-three deer. They were all running. When the fog lifted, I could see why. From my little spot in the sunflowers, I could count eight other hunters on the flat expanse of the ranch. Everywhere the deer went, they ran into another hunter. It wasn't my idea of a hunt. I started to cry, walked to the house, and put my rifle away.

By January, I was beginning to feel pretty good. But I also hadn't figured on what the effects of pregnancy would do to the urinary system. When you have to go, you have to go—and you have to go all the time.

We went snowmobiling at the cabin for New Year's. It seemed that I spent most of the week stopping my sled for an emergency trailside pit stop. Having to extricate yourself from a bulky snowmobile suit and all the clothing inside it next to the side of a snowmobile trail is not fun. One of my most embarrassing moments in the outdoors came during one of those situations that week. Somehow, in the urgency of the situation, I didn't get all the bulky clothing properly gathered up out of the way. Bluntly, I peed right in my snowmobile suit. Outdoorswoman-Supermom was not off to a roaring start.

In June our beautiful daughter, Shannon, was born. Determined to raise her with an appreciation of the outdoors, I carried her around the yard the day we arrived home from the hospital. At each tree, I lifted her close, touched a leaf to her tiny hand, and told her the name of the tree. Now that she was here, I planned to continue my outdoor activities unabated. She would just come along.

"Life isn't really going to change. There will just be one more participant," I thought foolishly.

There was one more delightful little participant, but things did change. Whereas we used to keep a pretty loose schedule, catering to each other, now we had to keep a pretty rigid schedule, both of us catering to Shannon.

There is a certain level of reality about the practicality of taking a six-month-old baby deer hunting that is lost on anyone who has never been responsible for a small child. Still, Shannon did go deer hunting that first year. Stan and I took turns staying with her. Pat Empson sat with her one day so Stan and I could hunt together. Stan even took her for a stroll in the woods in her baby backpack. We were still going outdoors, we were simply adjusting the level of intensity.

When Shannon was just a few months old, we moved from the Field Ranch to the Humphrey Farm, which was only a few miles away. We were now into potato farming in a big way—three thousand acres of potatoes and vegetables. We rented most of the acreage, but the Humphrey Farm was a purchase. The day we moved into the white house with the two red Dutch roof barns, settled among the oaks and butternuts, I told Stan, "I hope that my next move is when they carry me out feet first." I was home.

The Humphrey Farm was a lovely outdoor setting. We made loop walking trails in the woods on either side of the house. At first, I carried Shannon on walks down those trails. Later, she would toddle down them on some of her first tentative steps. That is about as out-doors as I got to go most of the time. I was a working mother, and I felt guilty picking up my bow or gun when I got home from work. It seemed that I should spend time with Shannon. In fact, I wanted to spend time with Shannon. Reality was that I had to adjust my level of activity to fit with my role as a mother.

Shannon must have been about thirty months old when I decided it was time to try bowhunting with her. One warm September after-noon, I came home from work, put on my camo, took Shannon and my bow, and headed for a fencerow on the back of the farm. There was a row of trees between our place and the neighbors, where the deer liked to cross. I did not really expect to shoot anything and prob-ably would not have with a child as small as Shannon along, but I thought we might see some up close.

Shannon chattered and wiggled incessantly.

"Shh!" I whispered. "You'll scare the deer and bunnies."

"SCARE THE DEER AND BUNNIES!" she exclaimed loudly while laughing.

We decided to abandon bowhunting and go for a walk.

Dark Days
· · · · · · · · · · · · · · · · · · · ·

In 1985 it seemed that our whole world began to unravel, outdoors and in. The price of potatoes dropped to fifty cents for one hundred pounds, a low practically unprecedented. Eventually we would lose the farm and the cabin would be sold to generate a down payment on a house in town. I would take a leave of absence from my job to work on a doctoral degree and Stan would go to law school. Like many farmers, we would leave the land. Luckier than many, we were able to hold our lives together and would be able to start a new life in a different direction.

Losing the cabin was the hardest part for me. The Empsons and the Kalmbachers both offered to help make the payments on it so we could keep it. It just wasn't a realistic possibility. We needed the cash we could get out of it. In the end, Stan spared me the pain of moving out. He rented a truck and made the last trip to the cabin by himself. Since he is a very quiet, private person, I will never know what he thought about that day.

We left most of the furniture. He did bring back the Amish rocking chairs, the coyote rug, the kerosene lantern that had been a gift from the Kalmbachers, and the wolf print that the Empsons had given us. We put them in the family room of our new home in Plover so it would feel like the cabin as much as possible.

That first deer season without the cabin was really hard. Stan was living in St. Paul, attending law school, and did not plan to go hunting. Elaine and Jim Kalmbacher put in with me for permits to hunt at the Sandhill Wildlife Area. We all drew permits, and Elaine drew a buck permit. The hunting area is managed for large bucks, so we all hoped Elaine would have a chance for a big one.

It was awful. The hunting area was crowded. We did not see any deer. Some "hunter" shot at Elaine. We ate Thanksgiving dinner at home for the first time in fifteen years.

The second deer season started out worse. It would be the last year that we would have the farm. We were still operating it while Stan finished law school, though we were not living there. Stan was not planning to hunt. None of our regular deer hunting party would be together.

This would be the first deer season I would miss since I started back in the early seventies. I was depressed. In fact, I was positively groveling in self-pity.

Bonnie Clark and her husband, Arlyn, had hunted deer on our farm since we purchased it. Their prime motivation for hunting was the meat. Certainly that was easy enough to fulfill on the Humphrey Farm. They harvested at least one deer each year.

I am motivated more by the social aspects of deer hunting. Not that I don't like the venison. Venison alone would not keep me deer hunting.

"Why don't you come down to the farm with us tomorrow," Bonnie offered before we left the office on Friday afternoon before opening day.

Bonnie and I have been close friends for fifteen years. It's a different relationship than many women have. We don't do lunch. What we do is seek the other one out when the chips are really down. We know that we can count on the other one to listen, and no matter how hard it is to give an honest reaction to the problem, we know the other one will be brutally honest and that the conversation will be completely confidential. It is good to have a friend like that.

"No, I'm too depressed," I moaned. "I wouldn't enjoy it anyway."

"If you change your mind, give us a call."

For some reason, I did change my mind. Maybe I couldn't stand to be like Kit, our old springer spaniel, sulking by the back door the opening day of the first pheasant season that she could not go. I called Bonnie and asked if she and Arlyn would pick me up on the way down. Stan planned to stay home with Shannon. He had studying to do anyway.

We arrived at the farm well before daylight. Bonnie and Arlyn had permanent tree stands built in the woods. Not one to sit in a tree after my bear hunting experience, I plunked down under a huge white pine that marked the corner of the woods. I faced the open field and waited for the fog to lift and the sun to rise. That is one of the things about deer hunting. There is plenty of time to think.

That morning I reflected on another year that Bonnie and Arlyn had come down to the farm to hunt. We were still living in the Humphrey house then. Times were better and maintaining a sense of humor was easier. Bonnie mentioned at the office one day that the worst part about hunting at our place was that there really wasn't any good way to answer the "call of nature." Of course this is something of a universal complaint of outdoorswomen. The fly on your jeans just doesn't serve the same purpose for women that it was designed to serve for men. In the case of our woods, there were so many neighboring men hunting close to the line fence that there just wasn't a spot out there where you could be assured of any privacy.

Stan and I got to laughing about Bonnie's plight one night at supper and cooked up a practical joke to play on her. The next day I went to the lingerie department at Shopko, a local discounter. I picked out the most sleazy negligee I could find. It was purple lace. When I went through the checkout counter, the clerk held it out at arm's length by the thumb and forefinger of each hand. Trying not to look too disgusted, she commented, "I didn't even know we carried anything like this."

At home that evening, Shannon, then about three years old, "modeled" the tacky item over her Oshkosh bibs. We took pictures before we wrapped the "gift." The night before deer season, we drove out to the woods and trudged through the deep, powdery snow, our breath crystallizing in the frigid air.

"I hope she is too preoccupied to notice our footprints when she walks in tomorrow," I commented.

Late in the day on Saturday, Bonnie and Arlyn drove in with two deer in the trunk.

"Looks like you guys did well," I said enthusiastically.

"I guess I could have done even better," Bonnie said laughing.

She took out the purple evening attire and showed us the gift the neighboring hunters had left in her tree stand. In it had been a note that said, "If you get cold around mid-morning, put this on and come over and visit."

"I was so embarrassed, I didn't know what to think," Bonnie chuckled. "I just knew they were all looking at me, waiting for a reaction."

She never knew we had done it until some months later, when I had a stack of "Shannon" photographs to show off at coffee break. When I passed the pictures around the lounge, I didn't realize that the purple nightie pictures were in the stack. It didn't take Bonnie long to realize that she had seen that item somewhere before.

As the fog lifted on the field in front of me, I saw several deer move across. They were all does and were running besides, so I did not lift my rifle. About 9:30 A.M. I became bored, cold, and hungry. If I moved around the woods, I would disturb everyone else. So I went back to the truck and ate part of a box of Girl Scout cookies and drank some coffee. Bonnie joined me after a bit. No coffee for her though. She did not want to make a nature call, especially after her earlier experiences.

Around 10 A.M., I went into the woods and hunkered down under a maple tree. To my amazement, just fifteen minutes later, a young buck came trotting out in front of me. I raised my rifle and fired. He ran a few yards and dropped. Bonnie and Arlyn came over and Arlyn field-dressed him. We decided to leave him where he was so the others could resume the hunt.

I sat under my tree for the balance of the day. I was glad to have the venison, but my thoughts were not focused on that. I thought about the events of the past three years. I thought of the changes that had been forced upon us. Some would ultimately be for the better, but who could see that at the time? I would finish my doctoral degree the following spring. That fall, I was in the throes of writing my PhD dissertation. Dan Trainer had been encouraging me to do that almost from the day he first knew me. It took the crisis of losing the farm to nudge me into starting the process. My thoughts that day were not of the future, however, but of the pain of the past and present. I am sure that I cried a few times as I sat there in the snow.

Even in the blackest days, however, there had been the glimmer of hope. Even in the saddest moments there had been opportunities for laughter and the renewal that can bring. One such event occurred the last time that Shannon and I went to the cabin on a mother/daughter trip. I was on break from my classes at Madison. Stan was trying to hold the farm together. We had already listed the cabin with a realtor.

Going to the cabin at that point was like spending time with a dying person. You did all you could to enjoy what little time you had left.

One afternoon, while Shannon napped, I decided to steal a few moments of fishing on the dock. Fishing is a very relaxing activity for me, and the fish are almost beside the point. I took my rod down from the log rafter in the living room.

"This rod has quite a history," I thought to myself.

The summer of my sixteenth birthday I came into my first big money. I had a job babysitting a nine-year-old girl who lived across the lake. The aluminum boat was my transportation to work. At the end of the first week, I received $25. Cash in hand, I walked to Keego Harbor, entered the sport shop, and purchased what I thought was the most wonderful combination of fishing tackle in the world. The reel was a Mitchell 300, just like Dad's. He had a Shakespeare rod, but I liked the color of the Wright and McGill "Favorite 6½." It had vivid sapphire accent colors on the handle and wrapping. I still fish with this same rod today, after nearly three decades. About ten years ago, when the guides started to fall off, Stan took the rod to a rod maker in Minocqua and had ceramic guides and new wrapping put on. The rod was more beautiful than ever, except for the loss of the little eagle medallion that is the trademark of Wright and McGill. Recently, I had the chance to meet Lee McGill. He sent me a replacement medallion.

I carried the rod and tackle box down to the dock, tied on a chartreuse jig head, fixed a nightcrawler in place, and cast out in front of me. The late afternoon August sun was hot on my face. It was the late summer, intense heat that you soak up for all you are worth, because you know winter is coming.

The jig plunked in the still water. I cranked it in. I repeated this several times before a very large bass took the bait. He put up a good fight, but my trusty old rod prevailed. My only problem was how to land him. I had not taken a landing net down to the dock. When I got him up close, I reached down toward his mouth to pull him in by hand. That caused one last burst of energy. Mr. Bass gave a frantic lunge and broke the line.

I looked over my shoulder to see a man standing on the beach in front of Sportsmen's Paradise. He stood there shaking his head, apparently having observed the whole spectacle.

Undaunted, I tied on another jig, identical to the first, and cast out. Another huge bass hit the first cast and the fight was on again.

"Don't lose this one," the man on the beach kibitzed.

I wondered why the know-it-all didn't get a net instead of standing there flapping his jaw.

The struggle was like an instant replay of the previous encounter. Finally, I reached into the water to grab the fish. As I pulled up on the line with my right hand, the mouth of the fish gaped open, revealing two identical chartreuse jig heads hooked in its lips. I started to laugh and that moment's hesitation was just the opportunity that my adversary needed. He lunged and broke the line a second time. I sat there laughing while the man on the beach heaved a disgusted sigh, shrugged his shoulders, and returned to his cabin.

Back under my tree in the November deer woods of Wisconsin, the sun began to fade. I thought how much of the previous three years had been spent feeling like a dying person. The imminent loss of the cabin and farm permeated every event. Certainly a way of life had died, but somehow I had not. Here I was, trying desperately to continue activities that were important to me, activities that had become part of who I am, not just something I do.

Starting Over

. . . .

Stan and I both finished school in 1989. That year we took up camping. Shannon's friend, Mollie Sprouse, and her parents got us started with a short excursion to a nearby state park. We already had piles of camping gear, so that wasn't a problem. The girls had a great time, so we bought Shannon her own tent and went on several other excursions with the Kalmbachers and on our own. It was something we could afford to do and it was a way to get outdoors.

In the fall of that year, we planned to deer hunt in the Chequamegon National Forest. It would be the first time that the Empsons and Kalmbachers would both join us for deer season since we sold the cabin. We decided to rent a cabin in a totally new area. So, earlier in the fall, we made a scouting mission to northwestern Wisconsin.

One Friday in early October, we loaded our gear in the old Suburban and headed for the north woods. We had picked out a national forest campground on Moose Lake. The colors were brilliant that afternoon as we crossed the Wisconsin River near Wausau.

We arrived at the campground after dark. The leaf litter was thick and damp. It smelled so good—the sweet smell of newly fallen leaves.

We picked out a spot not too near to other campers and Stan and Shannon set up the tents. Little six-year-old Shannon was determined to sleep alone in her own tent. I started supper. We cooked venison steaks from the deer I had shot the year before, mushrooms, onions, and hash brown potatoes. It was cold, so Stan started a campfire in addition to the cooking stove. He opened a bottle of wine and we sat there in the chill night air under a nearly full moon, enjoying the bounty of the past deer season and thinking about the excitement of the season to come.

Early the next morning, I awoke to a mournful howling.

"What is that?" I asked, nudging Stan awake.

He couldn't hear it and it stopped in a few seconds. I forgot about the noise until later in the day.

We spent a glorious fall day in the woods. Topography maps in hand, we scouted every area that we could work into the schedule. We really did not see a great deal of deer sign, but what we saw looked promising. We saw some of the biggest buck rubs I had ever encountered. Shannon was finally getting big enough to appreciate the nature lessons that we had to offer on the hikes that we took.

At sunset, we drove back into the campground. What a sunset it was! The lake was magenta in the dying October light. The leaves were magnificent. The full moon was beginning to rise. We stopped the truck to pick up some dead wood for our night fire. Just at the moment we stepped from the truck, the howling started again.

"What is that?" I resumed my question of earlier.

It was not the usual yipping of coyotes.

"It must be wolves," I said excitedly.

I had never heard wolves before, but I knew that there was a pack in that general area. When I returned to work on Monday, I asked Professor Ray Anderson if I could borrow a tape of wolf sounds. That confirmed the suspicion of the weekend encounter.

The wolf music was a perfect symphony for the wine-colored skies and the full moon rising in the October evening. It was eerie and beautiful all at the same time. It is the only time that I have ever been lucky enough to hear it.

That deer season, Jim Empson and Stan started to discuss the possibility of an elk hunt. We knew we would need to start planning way ahead. None of us could afford to go at that time, but we decided to divide up efforts and begin to contact state fish and game agencies and outfitters.

Slowly, one excursion at a time, we moved back into our outdoor life. It was not the same life that we had had on our own farm and operating out of our own cabin. It did, however, offer some advantages. We were not tied to one place. We have had an opportunity to visit and experience new ecosystems and new places.

I learned a valuable lesson through all that happened in those years. You can love a place. You can even be shaped by a place, but you and place should not be one and the same.

I also learned to appreciate the wonderful legacy of our public lands. Not everyone can afford to own a cabin or hunting land. Not everyone can even afford the price of a resort or motel room. However, because of the farsightedness of those who came before us, every citizen in this country has a place to walk in the woods, a place where the wildlife and waters are held in public trust. Without the public lands, the wildlife would become an essentially private resource. Here in Wisconsin, we are very fortunate to have vast acreages of national, state, and county forests that we all can enjoy. We must protect them and manage them so that those of us who have invested in "grandmotherhood" will have a place to walk in the woods with our grandchildren.

The Cycle of the Hunt

. . . .

The last slide showed the pack string, loaded with meat and ant-lers, heading across the partially frozen creek. My voice cracked with emotion as the last sentence of my narrative died away. My face was flushed. Was it from the glass of wine that accompanied the elk steak dinner I had so carefully prepared for my guests?

The meal had been a labor of love. Every detail was planned meticulously: the linen tablecloth, the china and crystal, every accom-paniment prepared painstakingly from scratch. The ritual of the prepa-ration and sharing of the meat and the tradition of sharing the story are important. That telling, sharing, and eating completed one revolu-tion in the cycle of the hunt. The flush in my face was the resurfacing of the emotions I felt during the hunt.

The cycle began two years earlier with preparation for the hunt. I planned it along with my husband, Stan, and Jim Empson, a friend from Michigan. We had whitetail hunted together for years. This was to be our first elk hunt.

I am a worrier. So the first emotion was apprehension mixed with excitement. It doesn't take much to start me worrying, and this adven-ture had plenty of fodder for the worry mill. How would we pay for it? Would I be able to meet the physical challenge? Would the horses be unmanageable? Would I shoot well enough?

One particular apprehension was that as a woman I might not be truly welcome in camp. Of course, I never believed that any outfitter would be crass enough to say I wasn't welcome, but when Dave Hettinger said that Selway-Bitterroot Outfitters would love to have me, I worried still.

With the question of the outfitter settled, we turned our attention to preparing ourselves. All summer and fall we trekked faithfully to the shooting range every weekend. We honed our shooting skills. We experimented at the loading bench.

All summer, I biked and walked in preparation for the hunt. I should have biked and walked more. I knew the hunt would be physically challenging, but I had no idea how challenging.

We read books and articles about elk, elk habitat, and elk hunting. I passed up an opportunity to buy a quarter of beef from a colleague. Instead I studied elk recipes in my game cookbooks.

When the day of departure finally arrived, the emotion was excitement. After all the planning and preparation, we were finally underway. But, as the miles ticked away and the Idaho border loomed closer, the old worries flooded in and I became more and more apprehensive.

By the time we met our outfitter for breakfast that first morning, I was downright sick to my stomach. The first person we met was Darrel Johnson, the camp cook. My nervousness subsided a little as he shook my hand. He had big warm hands and a smile to match. Still, as we met the rest of the crew and ordered breakfast, I chose oatmeal and only ate half the bowl.

It was raining on the flats in Hamilton as we loaded into the trucks and headed to the high country. The elevation changed the character of the precipitation. Every mile brought deeper snow. The contrast with the dreary, rainy morning that we left behind was stark. At the trailhead, the corral timbers had six inches of snow on them. The flocked fir trees reminded me of a Christmas card scene. The red plaid of the wrangler's wool vest was a spark of color as he moved among the stock he rounded up.

At noon, we mounted our horses and embarked on the three-hour ride to camp. As we headed to the pass that would take us to our creek-bottom destination, my stomach settled, my worries subsided, and the intense beauty of the scenery carried me away. The emotion was awe.

As we worked our way up the trail, the sun burned through the clouds. The trees were laden with heavy snow. At certain vantage points, I could see the length of the valley. The steep mountain slopes cascaded toward one another. Their heads were shrouded in snow squalls, their rocky feet cooled by the incessant flow of East Moose Creek. I felt very small and insignificant.

This was my first "designated wilderness" experience. My first trip to a place where "man (woman) is a visitor and shall not remain." Signs of the permanent residents were everywhere. We saw tracks of bear and mountain lion in the snow along the trail. We saw our first herd of elk on a mountainside. The group included several cows and one small bull.

As the trail descended to the creek bottom, the snow-laden spires of evergreens were replaced by the skeletons of trees. Three years earlier, at the time of the now famous Yellowstone fire, 14,000 acres of this drainage had burned in a one-day conflagration. I was glad that I had known we would be camping in a burn. Like most people, I would have expected the "big tree" picture-postcard version of wilderness. Over the course of the hunt, I came to appreciate the burn's stark beauty. New life sprouted everywhere on the forest floor; the Phoenix of succession rising from the ashes of charred trees.

As the horses splashed across the creek and into camp, the solitude and accompanying introspection of the ride ended abruptly. Everyone pitched in to put the camp in order. Still, at the lower elevation of the creek bottom, the precipitation was rain. The rain in the late October afternoon coupled with the tree skeletons, the ubiquitous soot, and the soggy soil had a dampening effect on my spirits. The supper conversation had the same effect. Not that it wasn't upbeat, but it was hunting-camp conversation. I had never considered the substance of hunting-camp conversation before. What makes it so generally enjoyable is a shared history—a knowledge of past deeds, place names, and a common experience. We were not yet privy to any of these. I felt like an outsider. I wondered if it is important for men to feel they belong to the hunting group.

The outfitter guided me the first day. We rode about an hour from camp. I was glad not to ride farther. My backside and knees were very sore from the previous day's ride. As we prepared to ascend the steep slope, Dave gave me preliminary instructions, "You don't need to be fast, but you need to stay with me. I'll go slow enough for you to keep up."

"Keeping up" sounded easy enough. Accomplishing it turned out to be another matter.

The slope was steep enough that we had to "switch back" up its face. The steep slope was complicated by snow-covered rocks. Try as I might, I could not stay on my feet. I slipped and fell repeatedly. At first this embarrassed me.

"It's not your ability," Dave said. "You have the wrong kind of soles on your boots."

The slipping was very inefficient. It took a great deal of effort to climb when I had to spend part of my energy recovering from each successive fall. Eventually, the tension started me laughing. My laughter infected Dave. It took four hours to reach a spot where we could glass the opposite mountain. "Serious glassin'," Dave called it. (My first bit of shared hunting-camp lingo.)

My pace was part of the reason for our slow progress. The other part was that we kept running into mule deer. About 10:30 A.M., we saw a nice buck about 150 yards away. He was a 4x4 with about a twenty-inch spread. My heart beat faster. I removed my scope caps and looked at him. Dave and I discussed whether or not I should shoot him. I debated. I have never had the luxury of such a protracted decision-making process while whitetail hunting. Either you do it or you don't have another opportunity.

"I'm going to let him go," I finally decided.

By noon I had passed three bucks. We had seen sixteen deer altogether. As we sat by a lunch fire, we watched three mountain goats walk along a ledge. I had never seen one before. What a luxury to spend an afternoon feeding a mountainside fire and watch those magnificent white, wooly creatures amble nimbly along the sheer rock! That one moment made the whole trip worthwhile.

Little snow squalls drifted across the mountains all afternoon. We glassed the opposite slopes and spotted sixteen cows. At about 4:15 P.M., we saw a huge bull. "He is at least a six," Dave said. "Do you want to go after him?" I knew I was too slow to get down one mountain and up the other before dark.

Coming down from the mountain was a trial. My knees, already sore from the horseback riding, strained with each step. At the foot of the mountain I struggled to get on the horse. The ride was torture. My short-legged gelding, Red, tended to trot. Each step he took in that gait jarred my already strained knees. Tears welled up in my eyes. I fought them back. At camp I suffered what I thought would be the ultimate embarrassment when I couldn't step down from the stirrups. I pulled one leg gingerly over the horse's back and took my other foot out of the stirrup. I dismounted (if you could call it that) by sliding down the horse's belly. My knees barely held when I hit the ground.

"I'm really hurting, Dave," I said when I headed for the tent. It wasn't a complaint, simply a statement of the true situation.

By Wednesday night I was pretty well into the swing of things. I had begun to feel like part of the camp, and I am not sure whether my muscles were any less sore or whether I was just used to hurting all the time. Dave announced it was time to switch guides and hunters, which they did every two days to keep things interesting. Dave paired up everyone else and I looked at Jeff Freeman and said, "Looks like it's you and me baby." We both laughed. I am not sure when I first sat next to Jeff at a meal, but we hit it off right away. He always offered me snuff and I always declined. We both always laughed. Shared humor is another way that bonds develop in hunting camp.

We left camp Thursday morning in a snowstorm. Not far along, a bull and cow moose crossed our trail. Even though I have spent many hours in the woods, I am always amazed when I see large game animals close up. For some reason, my first reaction is always disbelief. "They can't be real," I tell myself. The moose were a truly pleasant surprise. I took them for a good omen for the day.

We rode on, and before long Jeff stopped his tall mule and dismounted. He had spotted a bull, but I couldn't see it.

"He's up on the shelf," he said. "Do you want to go after him?"
I nodded.

We tied up our mounts and headed up the adjacent mountain. The objective was to get above the bull and spot him on the shelf. We would have to cross a slide between the mountains to reach the animal.

We really didn't have a great vertical distance to travel, perhaps 1,500 feet. The problem was the very steep slope, which was covered with rocks and snow. Jeff broke the trail and I matched his footprints step for step. I was so intent on keeping up that whenever he stopped, I bumped into him and we laughed. I fell often; Jeff carried my rifle so my hands would be free. When it was too steep to walk, I crawled on my hands and knees. When it was too steep or slippery to crawl, Jeff would give me a hand up. When we climbed high enough to look down on the shelf, the bull had disappeared.

"I know he's still there," Jeff said. "I really did see a bull." His blue eyes danced. He grinned under a heavy blond mustache.

I never thought otherwise. By this time I was exhausted. Even though the morning was cold and the snow was falling, perspiration was running down my face. I was so hot! I peeled off my wool cruiser, goose-down vest, and fatigue sweater. By the time I got down to my long underwear, Jeff must have wondered when I would stop. Later this got to be a joke around camp.

"We have a choice," he said. "We can either cross that rockslide and get over on the shelf where I saw him or we can go back down."

I looked at the treacherous terrain and noted that it looked like a hard trip. On the other hand, if the bull was still there, at least we didn't have far to climb. I didn't say anything, but simply nodded in the direction of the slide.

"Good girl," he said. "I didn't think you were a quitter."

We started the climb across the snow-covered rocks on the slide and Jeff took my hand to help me across the most treacherous places. When we reached the shelf, he suggested that we stop and build a lunch fire.

"We'll stay here and glass for the rest of the afternoon. There won't be anything moving around till later."

He didn't need to ask me to help collect kindling and firewood. I performed the task, and before long we had a blazing fire going on the uphill side of a large rock. We used the rock for a backrest and spent the afternoon telling stories, glassing the surrounding area, and getting to know each other.

I really enjoyed the opportunity to argue about resource management issues. We discussed wilderness management and the regulations that outfitters need to adhere to. We argued about the value of biodiversity in ecosystems and the merits of the wolf reintroduction idea. We talked about timber management in the national forests. It was an enjoyable way to spend an afternoon. "I told Mark I was going to get my bull on Halloween," he said.

"Oh, it is Halloween," I said. Over the week, I had lost track of time. I hoped he was right about it being our lucky day, but I figured the bull was long gone.

As the afternoon drew to a close, I stood up and expressed concern about descending the mountain in the dark.

"Just a few more minutes," Jeff implored, "or we'll waste everything we've already done. We'll wait till it starts to get dusk and then we'll hunt down the mountain as long as we have light."

Finally he stood up and we headed out. We hadn't gone twenty-five yards when he handed over my .308 rifle and pointed at the edge of the shelf. Two mule deer ears poked above the edge. A doe and two fawns joined us on the shelf and headed off toward the rockslide. Jeff blew once on his cow elk call. The deer didn't pay any attention, but a loud "THUMP" "THUMP" drew our eyes to the west, where another doe was headed toward us. It ran past, not four feet away, and joined the other deer.

"That's incredible," I whispered as Jeff turned, wide-eyed, toward me. He pointed up the shelf behind me, where six cow elk headed toward the slide. He blew once on the call. Five of the cows kept going, but one turned back.

"She's looking for something," he whispered, "Let's go that way."

We took two steps and another elk stood up. I confess that I don't know whether our ensuing conversations were shouts or whispers, but I said, "It's the bull!" as I fumbled with my scope caps.

"Shoot! Shoot! He's a good one," Jeff said.

I got the rifle ready, and I'm not sure if I sat down or if Jeff pushed me down, but I raised the rifle to make a sitting shot. He knelt behind me and put his arms around my waist so I would have a rest.

"Shoot! Shoot!," he urged.

I put the crosshairs on the bull's chest area and realized I was still wearing my snow-encrusted gloves. I had trouble getting my finger on the trigger. When I squeezed off, the shot was a little low. The elk dropped immediately but stood back up and stumbled. A second shot finished him. I pride myself on my marksmanship ability and wish a second shot had not been necessary.

Jeff reached the bull first. I ran down the hill as fast as possible to keep up. I slid on my rear part of the way because it was faster. When I reached him, I was excited, exhausted, snow covered, and sweating.

I put my arms around Jeff's neck, buried my face in his coat, and cried, oblivious to what he might think of me. I cry every time my hunt results in a kill. I can't explain this. I was glad Jeff didn't ask me to.

I am a fairly small person, five feet two inches and 115 pounds, and I don't do physical work for a living. So packing the elk out, which we did the next day, was a major challenge and an all-day job for Jeff and me. We had two pack mules, but the mountain was too steep for them to scale. The day was cold, the carcass was already frozen. My job was to start and tend a warming fire and assist with the skinning and quartering where I could. This is part of the cycle of the hunt, but my least favorite part. Downing a large game animal creates a huge job in the skinning, quartering, transporting, and processing of the carcass. These not-too-romantic jobs are as necessary to the completion of the cycle as purchasing a license. Even though the major work in this case was done by the guide, there is still, for the person who is acclimated to purchasing meat from the supermarket, that uncomfortable period when you have to deal with an animal that is no longer living but not quite meat. As we rode into camp that afternoon, with the quarters neatly tied in canvas, the emotion was satisfaction and relief.

The last day of the hunt was extremely cold; far below zero. Jeff has a saying: "Every day is another picnic on a stump" (more shared camp lingo). I told him that I wasn't too serious about filling my mule deer tag. I suggested going out for a "picnic on a stump" and then hunting for mulies in the late afternoon.

So we headed out at mid-morning. We rode about an hour down the trail, found a sunny spot, and built a lunch fire. We spent the midday cooking lunch, telling hunting stories, and rehashing our hunt. We watched a mountain goat and spotted a bald eagle during the course of the afternoon.

About mid-afternoon we headed back toward camp, glassing for mulies along the way. We hadn't gone far when Jeff spotted a group of them about 150 yards off the trail. We tied up our mounts. I removed my scope caps and we watched them. There were two bucks in the group. They were frisking around and trying to attract the attention of three does. Either one would have been an easy shot.

"What do you think?" Jeff asked.

"I think it's been a good hunt, they're having a good time, we've had a good day; so let's go back to camp and call it good."

We did.

I had already received the gift that would complete the cycle of the hunt. I didn't need more.

Back in Wisconsin, the glow of the last slide lit the faces of my guests, and as my voice cracked, I could see my emotion reflected by their eyes. They had been with me on the hunt. As the cycle of the hunt was complete, it began anew. The emotion of the magnificent scenery, the majestic animals, the shared experiences, kindled my hope for another opportunity to hunt. As the light of the slide died away and my guests sat quietly, I wished them wilderness. I wished wilderness for myself.

Dirt Is Our Friend

. . . .

I was definitely hooked on elk hunting. My passion for elk in-
spired me to join the Rocky Mountain Elk Foundation, an organization dedicated to the preservation and management of wildlife habitat.
I belong to many conservation groups. It is one way to give something
back to the land.

That first elk hunt changed my life. Future expenditures would
be judged by how long they would delay the next elk hunt. It would
take four more years to be in a financial position to go again.

In 1994 I started the search for an outfitter in New Mexico. We
thought we'd like to try some warmer-season elk hunting. Through a
series of personal recommendations, we found an outfitter who seemed
to fit the bill. Since I want to tell this story, yet my intention is not to
harm the individuals involved, the names of guides and outfitters in
this chapter are fictitious.

After checking out the references on Alex Guide and Outfitter, I
called Alex.

"Hi," I said cheerfully over the phone. "I'm Christine Thomas
and I am calling to discuss the possibility of hunting with you. I would

like to come down for the first rifle hunt. Do you have room for my husband and me?"

"Well," Alex drawled slowly in a cowboy sort of way. "Does your husband want to hunt too?"

There was a long silence. I repeated the question to Stan, who was listening in from the adjacent chair. He scowled at the inquiry.

I started to laugh and Alex laughed as well. I liked Alex.

The next morning over coffee I asked Stan what he thought about elk hunting.

"I would love to go, but I think it's a lot of money. We have an income-tax bill due in two weeks."

I was tight-lipped for the rest of the day.

That was Wednesday. Saturday, I called Alex and booked a hunt. I was in the middle of a contract research project for the National Bowhunter Education Association and would use the extra money from that.

Of course, we still had to draw licenses for the Gila Wilderness area. Alex had already sent us the applications. I signed Stan's name to his and mailed them with a check for the fees.

I did not tell Stan I had done any of this. Maybe I wouldn't have to. We weren't that likely to get licenses. It was about a fifty-fifty chance, and if we did draw, how disgruntled could he be? Who would complain about a wife who forced him to go elk hunting?

A week or two passed. I was euphoric. It was a wonderful, delicious secret. I liked the excitement of just being in the running for a license. One night, as Stan and I sat eating supper on the deck, he looked over at me and said, "You booked a hunt, didn't you?"

"What makes you think so?"

"I can read you like a book," he commented.

He was pretty quiet about the situation, but then he is pretty quiet about most situations.

The weeks passed. Finally it was the morning that the license information would be available on a 900 number. We sat down for coffee, when I remembered that we could call in to receive the news.

"Why don't you bring the phone here?" Stan said.

"A positive sign," I thought. I understood that he wanted to share my reaction.

I dialed the 900 number. Then I punched in the code on my license application.

"You have drawn a license for unit . . . ," the electronic voice on the other end of the phone reported.

"We drew! We drew!" I exclaimed excitedly.

"You are a beautiful woman," Stan said as he hugged me.

Things were going great. I was really feeling independent.

"What a long way I've come," I thought. "I did this myself. I made decisions. I took affirmative action without seeking approval or without letting all my insecurities get in the way."

I was feeling pretty grown up.

One of my research checks arrived just in time to pay the outfitter. The deposit was $2,500.

Then the liability waiver arrived in the mail. It was very troublesome. Basically, it said that even if the outfitter did not show up for the hunt that we could not recover our deposit. It actually said that if we died from food poisoning we would have no recourse. We couldn't even sue him if he shot both of us.

I did what I always do when I see a confrontation coming. I ignored it. I set the form aside and pretended that it did not come. A month went by. The outfitter wrote me a letter asking if I had received the forms and enclosing another copy.

Stan refused to sign the form. He is a contract attorney who specializes in insurance defense.

"This is the most one-sided contract I have ever seen," he lectured one evening.

I called the outfitter to discuss our concerns. I started this, so it seemed that I should be the one to pursue it.

Eventually, I could see that Stan needed to be the one to take it over. If he had not been an attorney, I would have needed to hire one. Still, I didn't feel grown up or independent anymore.

The weeks dragged on. The outfitter's insurance company refused to modify the form. We refused to sign it. The outfitter refused to take us hunting if we did not sign. I was so frustrated and disappointed.

"This is not what elk hunting is supposed to be about," I said one evening. "Elk hunting is supposed to be about habitat, wild country, elk, excruciating physical exertion, friendship, and spirituality."

We were mucking around with lawyers and insurance companies. Something was wrong with this picture.

Three weeks before the hunt, we mutually agreed that we could not work together. He sent us our money back and I was looking for another outfitter. We knew we were not likely to get anyone that good on such short notice, but I started the search.

The search was exhausting. Finally, I had two options. I chose Craig. We knew we were going to get to spend five days hunting elk in a wilderness area. That is the most we could count on.

Still, I was excited. One of the most exciting things was that I could buy a bear license if I wanted. Another decision. I swayed back and forth. Craig told us that they had not seen that many bear, but that it was my choice. Finally, Stan bought the license for me. The decision was made.

We met the outfitter and two guides and the two other hunters at the trailhead on the appointed day. I was pretty excited. The outfitter told us that bears had ransacked our camp two days before and that they had seen elk when they brought in camp supplies the day before. We saw a number of elk, deer, and turkey on our way up.

The guides saddled the horses and mules. I would be riding a bay mule named Ruby. Stan got quite a kick out of the fact that I would be riding a mule.

Everything was about set when the guides discovered that they did not have a bridle for Ruby. That meant they would need to drive back down to another trailhead and get one from the outfitter's truck. It would be a two-hour delay.

The other two hunters, guys from Kentucky, had never hunted with an outfitter before. They did not know what to think. Based on our one previous experience, we told them that "hurry up and wait" seems to be the order of the day. We sat there in New Mexico's warm late-October sun and enjoyed our lunches.

Finally, we headed into the Aldo Leopold Wilderness Area. Leopold, of course, is one of the most respected figures in conservation history. He worked much of his career in Wisconsin. I liked the idea of hunting in "his" wilderness area.

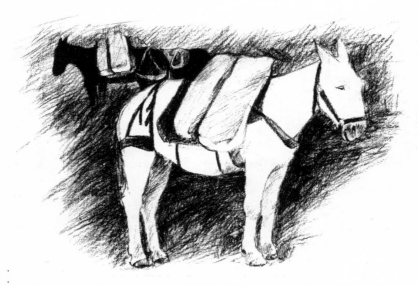

It was a fairly short ride to camp, just under two hours. The scenery was spectacular and nothing like I had ever seen before. The vegetation was vaguely familiar—arid climate adaptations of our more water-loving species. The student of habitats would have much to learn here. The wetter sides of hills had vegetation more like that in the northern west. Those slopes that faced the sun were covered with scrubby, shorter-needled plants. There were many species of conifers. They were green against a moistureless, intense blue sky. Mixed in were oaks that had tiny leaves that had turned bright-lemon yellow for autumn. At home, oaks do not turn yellow, so this was a very interesting phenomenon.

It was very dry and dusty. The area was in the midst of a drought that had lasted two years.

One thing that surprised me was that the area was full of fences, cow tracks, and cows. This was a U.S. Forest Service wilderness area. A place where "man is a visitor and shall not remain." The fences were an intrusion on the experience.

As I mentioned, there were two guides. One of them was a Mexican immigrant who had become a citizen of the United States. He spoke little English but understood it very well. He had a great sense of humor and would guide the Kentuckians. We would be guided by "The Jerk."

The Jerk looked like something right out of some western cattle drive movie. Not the young, dashing, Rowdy Yates type. More the forty-looks-sixty, weather-beaten, limps from too many horse accidents, couldn't keep from looking dusty if he tried type. To top it off, he was an expert on every subject that came up. He kept referring to the Aldo Leopold Wilderness Area as "our ranch," because he had formerly worked for the ranchers who had a cattle lease there. That really irked me, because "their ranch" belongs to all the citizens of the United States, managed in trust for all of us by the U.S. Forest Service. I wasn't too sure I wanted "my ranch" to be a ranch at all. Not the designated wilderness part of it, at any rate.

When we arrived at camp, The Jerk gave us the grand tour. This camp was very primitive compared to our posh accommodations in Idaho. Stan and I would share a teepee tent. The kitchen was outside. No cook tent. Just a fire ring, a tarp tied between a few trees, and a downed log to stack supplies on.

There were no "facilities." You just took a shovel out in the trees and used it to cover your droppings, cat-fashion.

None of this bothered me. I was prepared because I had called enough references to know what kind of camp we would be getting.

As we finished the tour, I got "the lecture." The Jerk looked right at me.

"See those water jugs?" he said, pointing to three five-gallon jugs. "That is all the water we have for five days. It is for drinking only. You can't use that water to wash your feet. I don't want to see you using that water for anything but drinking. This ain't no Hilton. You city people need to learn that dirt is our friend."

By the time he finished his little speech, he was shaking his finger in my face. I was humiliated. None of this was directed at anyone but me, and everyone knew it.

I decided not to comment. Instead I changed the subject.

"I have a bear license," I told The Jerk. "Craig said I could buy one and even said I would be doing him a favor if I took one out of this area. Bear season is open now. (Elk season opened the next morning.) I'd like to go sit down by the water tank until dark to see if one comes out." There were fresh tracks on the trail by camp leading to the mud hole where the cattle and all the wildlife in the area watered.

"This is an elk hunt," The Jerk lectured, again shaking his finger at me. "You do what you want, but if you shoot a bear on that tank and leave that stinking gut pile there, every elk in the country will leave and you will ruin the hunt for everyone."

What could I say? I went to my tent, sat on the ground, and lay my head on Stan's thigh. He did not say anything, which was fine. I could hear voices outside.

"I guess she didn't like my little water lecture," The Jerk was telling the guys from Kentucky.

I couldn't hear any comment from them, so I didn't know what they thought. I was so embarrassed by everything.

"Let's go for a walk," Stan said.

We walked on beyond the camp. Neither of us said anything. Finally, Stan sat down on a log and I sat next to him. My whole body began to shake. My throat knotted up. Tears welled up in my eyes. I fought them back, but they flowed down my face anyway. I was angry. So angry. I did not say a word, but I thought, "Who is this asshole and why am I paying him $2,000 to treat me like a twelve-year-old?"

Of course I didn't want to ruin anyone else's hunt. I wouldn't do anything to detract from anyone else's experience if I could help it. It was The Jerk's attitude toward me that I could not stomach.

As the tears fell, Stan brushed one away and then held my hand. He didn't need to say anything. I knew he understood what was going through my mind.

I decided that I was not going to let The Jerk ruin my hunt. I had waited for four years for this. I was in one of the most beautiful places on earth, and I was going to get the most out of it that I could. I didn't know at that moment that we would not see an elk the whole season. It would not have mattered if I had. I resolved that I would get everything out of this experience that I could if I had to climb over the dead body of The Jerk to do it.

When the tears were gone we walked back to camp. I offered

to help make dinner. The Jerk indicated that I could peel the potatoes. I took my Buck knife out of its sheath and commenced peeling and slicing.

"So, I guess you're somebody famous or something," The Jerk said inquisitively.

The Kentucky hunters had recognized me from articles they had seen in outdoor magazines.

"I'm known in the outdoor community," I confirmed.

"So, you going to write an article about me?" The Jerk inquired worriedly.

"Count on it!" I said emphatically as I sliced the last potato.

The Jerk behaved much better after that.

Grunt!

. . . .

This past deer season was a special event. Our daughter, Shannon, completed Hunter Education and became a hunter. She was already an outdoorswoman and had participated in many hunts as a helper and a spectator. This year she was old enough to buy a license and to become a full participant. Pat and Jim Empson and the Kalmbachers joined us for the celebration.

We rented a really nice cabin near the Chequamegon National Forest, arranged to take Shannon out of school, and headed north for the full nine-day Wisconsin season.

It was a great season. Stan and Shannon saw the newly reintroduced elk one morning and heard wolves one evening. We all saw deer, and Jim Kalmbacher even got one. We had a wonderful Thanksgiving dinner and shared a great time with special friends. I had one of the most interesting experiences that I have ever had in the woods.

It was an early season. In Wisconsin the nine-day season always spans the Thanksgiving week. This year, because of the way Thanksgiving came in the calendar, deer season started earlier than most years. This meant that the deer were still rutting and the weather was better than usual.

The previous year, I had located a scrape along a trail that I thought looked pretty good, so a few days into this season, I decided to go back and take another look at the area. I walked into the trail on new snow. There were deer tracks everywhere. No other hunters had been in there during the season.

The trail goes over a rise and dips down into a low spot. There is relatively new-growth aspen in a clearcut to the west of the trail, tag alders to the east of the trail, and a cedar swamp beyond the alders. The trail goes straight up a fairly steep hill to the south. At the lowest point in the trail a large spruce tree sits just to the east, with branches that dip over the trail. That is the spot where I had seen the scrape the year before.

I walked to that spot and found that it was being actively used by a buck. There were tracks all around a scrape that was about three feet long and half as wide. It was completely free of the recent snow, and a spruce sprig had been torn from the overhanging branch and lay in the trail. This looked good to me. It was about mid-day when I happened on to this spot, and I was due back at the truck for lunch. I had never used scent before, but I had a bottle Stan had given me, so I put a few drops on the scrape and left behind an apple as well.

I had to find a good place to sit. There wasn't really anything ideal because it was so brushy. I did not want to sit right on the trail. About fifteen yards from the scrape I found a red pine that had a few small balsams around it for cover. I would be facing south, toward the hill. The trail was just a few yards to my right. I figured I would hunker down in that spot and hope for good luck. I went to join the others for lunch and returned for an evening set. When I returned that evening, the scrape had been worked over again, but the apple had not been touched. That night, I didn't see anything.

Wednesday afternoon I went back to the same spot. I arrived there about 3 P.M. I had barely sat down when I heard footsteps in the aspens to my right. The steps were coming quickly, and before I even had a chance to get nervous a doe stepped into the trail. She walked quickly to the scrape, followed by a small fawn. At the scrape, she barely hesitated and then went on up the hill and off into some slash on the side of the trail. Following right on their steps was a spike buck. He moved as quickly as they did, but hesitated for just a second longer at the scrape. I raised my rifle, but he was so close and the brush was so thick that I couldn't get a good sight picture. I suddenly realized that I had my scope turned up too high. I did have one opportunity to shoot but didn't want to take a chance on wounding him. He followed the doe and fawn up the hill and they all disappeared.

A few moments later, I heard some scurrying in the alders to my left. I looked over expecting to see a squirrel. Instead I was treated to the sight of a shiny, dark fisher slinking over downed logs. It was the only time I have ever seen a fisher in the woods. All in all, it was a good afternoon.

That buck that I had seen was definitely in the rut. He was after that doe, no doubt at all. I got to thinking that if the bucks were still rutting, maybe they could be grunted in.

I had never heard a buck grunt, nor had I heard a grunt call. That evening back at the cabin, I asked Jim Empson if he had one with him. He happened to have one in his truck, so he went out to get it and demonstrated it for me. It sounded like a low-toned pig snort to me.

The next morning was Thanksgiving. We usually go all out on that. Elaine and Shannon stayed in to help me cook. We baked cranberry nut bread, made cranberry sauce, and baked pumpkin and apple pies. Shannon made stuffed celery. We peeled potatoes, prepared stuffing, and stuffed a nearly twenty-four-pound turkey. We had the turkey in the oven at 11 A.M. We ate lunch, watched enough of the football game to be reasonably confident that the Lions were going to kill the Bears, and headed to the woods. Elaine and I went out alone that afternoon. Stan said he and Jim would follow when the game was over. He said he would meet me at our usual rendezvous point after shooting hours.

I returned to the scrape that I had been watching. It was a glorious afternoon. Not too cold and little or no wind. I like those quiet afternoons because I can hear for long distances. I sat down on a "hot seat," next to my red pine. I had a poncho liner in my pack, so I took that out, put it over my lap for extra warmth and to mask any movements I might make, and settled in for the afternoon.

Things were pretty dead. It was pleasant enough, but I could hear very well and nothing was moving anywhere. The time ticked by.

Finally, around 3:20 P.M. I became a little bored and got to thinking about that grunt call demonstration from the night before. I hadn't asked to borrow the call, because I thought maybe Jim was planning to use it. I figured I might be able to duplicate the sound without a call. I did feel a little self-conscious making wild noises out in the woods, but what the heck? No guts! No glory!

I made the best pig snort I could. Two of them. I wish I could describe this sound. I made it by drawing the air up out of the back of my throat, up through the sinus area behind my nostrils.

"SNORT." "SNORT."

Then I waited.

About three minutes later, I heard a swishing sound off in the alders to my left.

"Holy smokes!" I thought. "This really works."

I looked off in the direction of the sound, and a dark gray cat-like creature trotted out of the cedars into the alders. It looked huge. At first I thought it must be a mountain lion. Then I saw its bobbed tail and knew I had seen the first bobcat I had ever laid eyes on in the wild. It was magnificent. Every hair stood out of its body. Its coat undulated with its forward motion. The cat never varied its pace but trotted to within twenty yards of me, crossed the trail between me and the hill, and disappeared into the aspens to the southwest.

"Wow, that was cool!" I thought.

I waited ten minutes and decided to try that again.

"SNORT." "SNORT."

Instantly, I heard a swishing noise down in the cedars. I looked to my left and another bobcat came right out on the same trail as the first. This cat only came part way out into the alders. It stopped with a tree blocking my view of it, so I could not tell if I had spooked it. Then it turned on its own track and went back into the cedars.

I was so excited by those events that I didn't even wait until shooting hours were over. I packed up my stuff and went as fast as I could to tell Stan about what had happened. I must have looked like a drunk running down the hill to meet him at our rendezvous spot. By the time I got there I was giggling so hard about the ridiculousness of the interaction that I had just participated in that the tears were streaming down my face. My laughter was infectious, and Stan started to laugh too. Through my chuckling, I was finally able to get a sentence out:"You are never going to believe the story that I have to tell you!"

Stan staggered backward, braced himself against a tree, and said, "Okay, I'm ready."

About the Author

· ·

Christine L. Thomas is the sort of person with whom you could hunker down by the side of a trail, munch on a sandwich, and talk about everything from the deer stand you just left to the very funny joke you heard last night. Wife, mother, professor, outdoors adventurer, storyteller, and prankster, Chris is also the founder of the nationally acclaimed program, "Becoming an Outdoors-Woman." In 1996, the 3-day workshop drew more than 6,000 participants to 50 different sites in the United States and Canada.